# STENCILLING

furniture, home accessories and soft furnishings

# STENCILLING

## furniture, home accessories and soft furnishings

Decorate your home using stylish stencil designs:

over 30 practical projects, 400 inspirational photographs,

and easy instructions for all the basic techniques

Lucinda Ganderton

southwater

This edition is published by Southwater

Southwater is an imprint of Anness Publishing Ltd
Hermes House, 88–89 Blackfriars Road, London SE1 8HA
tel. 020 7401 2077; fax 020 7633 9499
www.southwaterbooks.com; www.annesspublishing.com

If you like the images in this book and would like to investigate using
them for publishing, promotions or advertising, please visit our website
www.practicalpictures.com for more information.

© Anness Publishing Ltd 2006

UK agent: The Manning Partnership Ltd
6 The Old Dairy, Melcombe Road, Bath BA2 3LR
tel. 01225 478444; fax 01225 478440; sales@manning-partnership.co.uk
UK distributor: Grantham Book Services Ltd
Isaac Newton Way, Alma Park Industrial Estate,
Grantham, Lincs NG31 9SD
tel. 01476 541080; fax 01476 541061; orders@gbs.tbs-ltd.co.uk
North American agent/distributor: National Book Network
4501 Forbes Boulevard, Suite 200, Lanham, MD 20706
tel. 301 459 3366; fax 301 429 5746; www.nbnbooks.com
Australian agent/distributor: Pan Macmillan Australia
Level 18, St Martins Tower, 31 Market St, Sydney, NSW 2000
tel. 1300 135 113; fax 1300 135 103;
customer.service@macmillan.com.au
New Zealand agent/distributor: David Bateman Ltd, 30 Tarndale Grove
Off Bush Road, Albany, Auckland; tel. (09) 415 7664; fax (09) 415 8892

ETHICAL TRADING POLICY
Because of our ongoing ecological investment programme, you, as our
customer, can have the pleasure and reassurance of knowing that a tree
is being cultivated on your behalf to naturally replace the materials used
to make the book you are holding. For further information about this
scheme, go to www.annesspublishing.com/trees

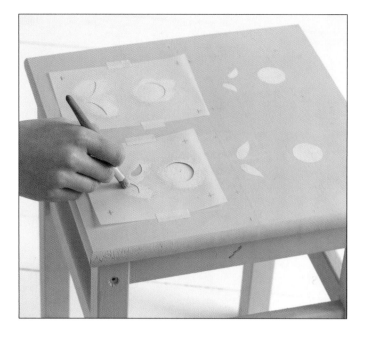

Publisher: Joanna Lorenz
Senior Managing Editor: Conor Kilgallon
Editors: Judy Cox, Felicity Forster, Doreen Gillon and Elizabeth Woodland
Additional text: Petra Boase, Emma Hardy, Sacha Cohen, Alison Jenkins,
Cheryl Owen, Liz Wagstaff, Stewart and Sally Walton
Special photography: Paul Bricknell, with additional photography by Tim
Imrie, Debbie Patterson, Graham Rae, Steve Tanner, Adrian Taylor
Stylist for special photography: Tamsin Weston
Designer: Bill Mason
Cover designer: Nigel Partridge
Production controller: Claire Rae

Previously published as part of a larger volume, *The Complete Book of
Decorative Stencilling*

10 9 8 7 6 5 4 3 2 1

PUBLISHER'S NOTE
The authors and publisher have made every effort to ensure that all the
instructions contained in this book are accurate and that the safest
methods are recommended. Readers should follow all recommended safety
procedures and wear protective goggles, gloves and clothing when
necessary and work in a well-ventilated area. You should know how to use
your tools and equipment safely and make sure you are confident about
what you are doing. The publisher and authors cannot accept liability for
any injury, damage orloss to persons or property as a result of using any
equipment in this book or carrying out any of the projects.

ACKNOWLEDGEMENTS
The projects were created by Lucinda Ganderton, with the following
exceptions: *Petra Boase:* Painted drawers (pp. 38–40), Leafy picture frames
(pp. 112–13). *Penny Boylan:* Citrus roller blind (pp. 78–9). *Emma Hardy:*
Organza cushion (pp. 66–7), Gilded candles (pp. 118–19). *Alison Jenkins:*
Rainforest curtains (pp. 73–5). *Cheryl Owen:* Scandinavian chair (pp.
35–7), Train toy box (pp. 41–3), Hawaiian hibiscus cabinet (pp. 44–7),
Daisy stool (pp. 51–3), African bedside chest (pp. 57–9), Striped table and
chairs (pp. 60–3), Dragonfly curtain (pp. 70–2), Leaf-etched vase (pp.
120–1). *Sandra Partington:* Elizabethan lampshade (pp. 104–5).
*Suzie Stokoe:* Summer quilt cover (pp. 84–6), Gold leaf picture frame (pp.
106–8). *Liz Wagstaff:* Gilded lampshade (pp. 102–3). *Stewart and Sally
Walton:* Bronze chair (pp. 32–3), Love pillows (pp. 92–3), Amish floorcloth
(pp.99–101), Framed chalkboard (pp. 109–11).

# CONTENTS

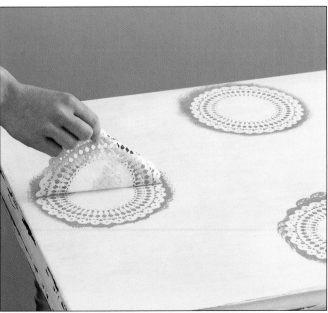

# INTRODUCTION

Stencilling is an enduringly popular art form, which is as fashionable now as it has been for many centuries. Versatile and adaptable, it has evolved alongside changing tastes in interior decoration, from Victorian Gothic to Bloomsbury bohemian, and new techniques and images are constantly being developed to fit in with current styles. After a decade of minimalism and plain walls, colour and pattern are once again finding their way back into our homes and interiors, and today's designers are once again reinterpreting traditional stencilling in an exciting new way. The most up-to-date stencils are both bold in design and colour and are graphic, with an unmistakably 21st-century look.

## SIMPLE STENCILS

Stencilling is straightforward, easy to put into practice and above all, great fun to do. The beauty of it, and much of the reason for its continued popularity, is that you can achieve professional-looking results very quickly and easily, without having any previous experience. There is great satisfaction in peeling back a stencil to reveal a crisply detailed one-off image, and also in building up a pattern or border from a repeated motif.

Fabrics, furniture and home accessories can be stencilled using the wide range of specialist paints available from The choices are endless and there is great scope for creativity. Depending on your own tastes, your time and your patience, you can decorate any surface in your home, from chairs, tables and cabinets to curtains, cushions and picture frames.

## USING THIS BOOK

This book is a comprehensive guide to stencilling techniques and an invaluable resource for anyone who is interested in stencilling, from the complete novice to the experienced crafter. The practical introduction covers everything you will need to know about cutting a stencil from card or plastic, and the different methods of applying colour by brush, roller or sponge to create various painted effects. There is a fascinating survey of historic stencilling styles, many of which are reflected in the projects, together with basic lessons in pattern making. The following chapters show you how to put all this information into practice and illustrate the vast potential of stencilled ornament in modern

design and interior decoration. The inspirational ideas range from gilded candles that can be finished quickly in an afternoon to bigger projects that may take a little longer to complete. From Rainforest Curtains and a Celtic Knot Box to an Elizabethan Lampshade and a Gold Leaf Picture Frame, you will find a wealth of projects to decorate.

## GETTING STARTED

Stencilling does not require much outlay of time or money. You may have some of the basic tools and art materials around the house, and acrylic paints are relatively inexpensive. New innovations such as the heat pen and easy-to-cut acetate have speeded up the process of making stencils from the days when they were hand cut from sheet metal, and photocopying saves a lot of time. Once you have chosen and made your first stencil, spend a little time experimenting with paint techniques and develop a few ideas of your own. All the projects have detailed instructions, which are fully illustrated with step-by-step photographs: you can follow these to the letter or use your own imagination to interpret the designs as you wish. Whatever the results, your stencilled creations will always be quite unique, as no two people will ever interpret a project in the same way.

*OPPOSITE TOP: Smarten up a simple kitchen chair with Scandinavian-style stencilling.*

*OPPOSITE BELOW: Classic motifs are ideal for a striking floorcloth.*

*RIGHT: Bold and abstract designs can enliven any window frame.*

# STENCILLING STYLES

The sheer versatility of stencilling means that it has appeared in many different guises over the years, and historic stencilling ranges from the purely functional to the highly decorative. Reverse stencil hand prints have been found in prehistoric cave dwellings, Egyptian tombs had stencilled patterning and Japanese fabrics were stencilled with "katagami" – resist floral designs. In the 1920s Mariano Fortuny recreated renaissance patterns on stencilled velvet and embellished them with Venetian glass beads. In more recent times it was even used as a propaganda medium by Italian fascists and Basque separatists, and hijacked by graffiti artists in Europe and America, whose paintings have developed into street art.

## PRACTICAL STENCILLING

Today stencilling is thought of as a purely decorative craft, but its origins are rather more utilitarian. In the early days of printing, it was the quickest and most effective method of colouring black and white wood block engravings and transferring designs on to fabric. Stencilled lettering has long been a quick method for manufacturers to transfer information on to packaging. The Shaker community used tin sheets pierced with fine lettering to label the vegetable seeds harvested from their fields and, in the 19th century, Italian fruit growers from the Mediterranean port of Sorrento developed the stencilled labels on their lemon crates into a fine art. Even today, stencils are used to mark crates of whisky in Scottish distilleries and wooden boxes of salted pilchards in Penzance, at the far west tip of England.

Stencilled design has also been used for adding pattern to domestic pottery, especially in France and Eastern Europe. Hungarian and Czech bowls of the mid-20th century were embellished with spot or border designs of flower baskets, fruit, vines and animals, in rich folk-art style. These designs were transferred by painting a coloured slip glaze through a stamped tin stencil, specially shaped to fit within the biscuit-fired dish. Three or more stencils could be used to build up the most detailed patterns. As technology advanced, the airbrush replaced the stencil brush, giving a smoother surface to the colour. The trompe l'oeil plate project is a witty re-interpretation of these popular ceramics.

## AMERICAN FOLK ART

Stencilled interiors reached their peak of popularity and expertise along the Eastern seaboard of the United States in the early 19th century. The elaborate wallpapers and woven carpets that settlers had enjoyed in Europe were no longer available, and home owners looked to paint as a way of creating decorative effects. Stencilling became a recognized trade and itinerant artists, such as J. Gleason of Rhode Island and Moses Eaton in New England, would travel from house to house, adding stencilled pineapples, garlands, swags and hearts to marbled and wood-grain effects.

*ABOVE: A simple fruit motif gives this tray a bright, tropical look, perfect for summer drinks or parties.*

*OPPOSITE: Floral motifs are always popular.*

Colour schemes, as now, depended largely on the taste of individual clients and ranged from subtle grey walls with simple repeated patterns to sunshine yellow with red and green flowers. Nowadays we go to great lengths to ensure patterns match exactly and that all our repeats line up, but surviving folk art walls were painted with a great panache that reveals a careless disregard for accuracy, visible brush marks and the occasional smudge.

## VICTORIAN GOTHIC

The Victorians used stencilling to add formal decoration to the interiors of public buildings such as churches, synagogues, stations, art galleries and town halls. Many of these original schemes have been refurbished to dazzling effect. As much surviving Victorian needlework and paintwork has faded over the decades, it is useful to remember just how bright the original threads and paints actually were. A recently discovered stencilling scheme of 1863 by Alexander Thomson (the leading Scottish architect of his day) shows a

surprisingly bright range of colours: Pompeiian red, bottle green and gold leaf. He included an eclectic combination of neo-classical, Asian and Egyptian motifs on the murals and borders of Lilybank House in Glasgow. Restoration work on London's Midland Hotel, built at the height of the railway boom, has revealed complex multicoloured stencilling schemes that originally extended down long corridors and across vaulted ceilings. Most of these were painted over by succeeding generations, for whom such intense pattern proved difficult to live alongside.

## ARTS AND CRAFTS

At the end of the 19th century, a new aesthetic movement transformed the decorative arts. Art nouveau, and the subsequent Arts and Crafts movement, was a fresh way of looking at natural subjects. Building on the inspiration of artists such as William Morris and the arts of Eastern cultures, the slavish realism and overblown ornamentation of the Victorian era was simplified into flowing, graceful forms. The stylized, two-dimensional patterns of this era were ideally suited to stencilling and with the growing enthusiasm for crafts, particularly among women, it became a highly popular method of decorating the home.

The advent of electric lighting meant that rooms were lighter and brighter than they had ever been, and the fussiness of the parlour

*ABOVE: Candles look stylish and fresh with the addition of a stencilled star motif.*

*RIGHT: Glass etching spray is a simple method of creating the illusion of etched glass.*

was gradually replaced by pale walls and uncluttered surfaces. The epitome of this new look was Charles Rennie Mackintosh's unique "Glasgow Style". Considered radical at the time, his elegant interiors are the precursor of late 20th century minimalism. He used stencilling as an unobtrusive way to add flat colour and pattern to canvas chair backs, bed hangings and upholstered seating. His favourite motifs of roses and sinuous plant forms have been much imitated and reproduced.

In America at the same time, larger scale stencils in a slightly softer style became highly popular. Continuous border designs encircled rooms, running both above and below plate and dado (chair) rails, and large friezes filled

the deep areas below picture rails. Single stencils, repeated motifs and overall patterns were all used, and stylized flora and fauna – birds, fish, insects and animals – were a favourite theme.

## ART DECO

As the soft lines of art nouveau gave way to the more angular shapes of art deco, so stencilled patterns changed. *The Practical Guide to Stencilling* by Frank Gibson, published in 1926, featured an array of motifs and all-over designs including the characteristic sunray pattern. Other enduring stencil designs – many of which appear in modern form in this book – included were Greek key borders, twining vines and bunches of grapes, fleurs-de-lys,

*ABOVE: Choosing pale colours for the stripes, shows up the bold stencil design on this quilt cover.*

*ABOVE RIGHT: Decorating your accessories in complementary tones will give a contemporary feel to the room.*

butterflies and (at the time when Tutankhamun's tomb was causing a sensation) an Egyptian scarab. The most intricate of all is a detailed reproduction of the willow pattern plate design in traditional blue and white.

Gibson's book suggests a wide range of textiles considered suitable for stencilling, which provide an interesting insight into the wide range of domestic linens to be found in an ordinary household. They include not just table cloths, but also runners, napkins and mats. Some of the decorated items are still to be found and many of them are still subjects for stencilling: lampshades, cushions, curtains and picture frames. Others – collar boxes, shaving paper holders, bookcase curtains and mantel borders – are now obsolete, but the idea of stencilling garden paling is charming and one that could be copied for a cottage-style plot.

## SWEDISH STYLE

One of the most influential decorating styles of recent years derives from the Gustavian look of 19th-century Sweden. The short days and long winters of Scandinavian countries mean that people spend a lot of time indoors, and interior colour schemes are predominantly pale in tone: cream, light blue and sage green provide the backdrop for highlights of dusky pink, cherry red and the favourite blue.

Artist Carl Larsson's book *My Home* introduced this style to a wider audience, who relished the detailed paintings of his wife and children in a house decorated with simple furniture, striped and checked fabric, and restrained stencilling. Small florals, looped ribbon bows, hearts and wheatsheaves all echo the embroidery designs of the period and region and were used on walls, floors and furniture. Any stencilling done in this style should be done in pale colours and gently aged by rubbing it lightly with abrasive paper to give an authentic look.

## CONTEMPORARY STENCILS

Interior design of the 1980s tended towards the flouncy and floral, and gave stencilling a reputation as fiddly and over-decorated. Since then, there has been a great turnaround in style. "New vintage" effects pay homage to the past, but are to be found in bright, clear shades with none of the fussiness of their original inspiration. Drawing on a wealth of historic decorative styles, new designers are reworking antique motifs such as oriental blossoms, paisleys and lace patterns in a bold, graphic manner, using new colours and shades.

The primary colours, flamboyant flowers and geometric patterns of 1970s wallpaper have already made a comeback, and they look more at home within the proportions of modern loft-style apartments and open living spaces than they ever did in suburban bedrooms and sitting rooms. These patterns are filtering through to stencil design, such as in the form of pop-art style canvases. By playing with scale – enlarging a single flower to cover a cushion – interior designers are creating a new, modern look.

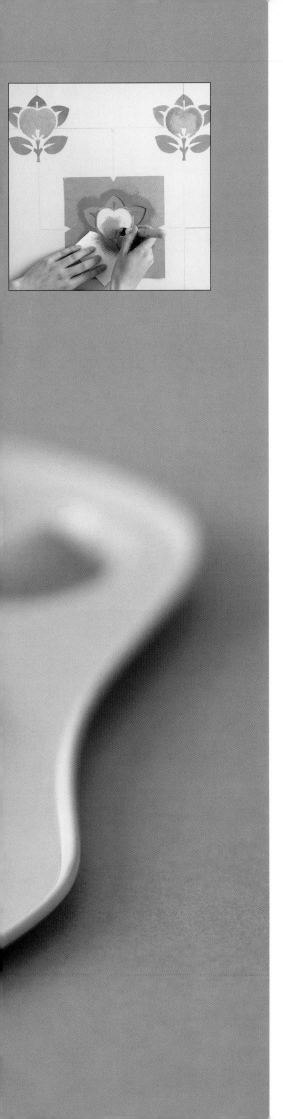

# STENCILLING BASICS

T he appeal of stencilling as a decorative technique lies in its immediacy. Getting started is easy, as it requires only a few basic materials and items of equipment, and no special painting skills. Even a complete beginner can achieve stunning results in a short time. The following pages show you how to make a stencil and how to use it, and suggest ways in which you can produce your own individual interpretations of the designs in the book to suit your own style and interior decoration.

*ABOVE: Making sketches and transferring your designs to stencil card or acetate can be very rewarding.*

*LEFT: Stencil brushes are available in many shapes and dimensions. It is important to clean them after every session to keep them in good condition.*

# STENCILLING EQUIPMENT

Making a stencil is a straightforward process that does not entail buying a huge amount of equipment. Some of the items you may already have around the house, and others are readily available from good art and craft suppliers. As with any other creative task, it is worth investing in the best tools for the job, in order to achieve a professional result. If you plan to make a lot of acetate stencils, for example, using a heat knife will save a great deal of time and a self-healing cutting mat is essential for safe stencil making.

## MEASURING AND MARKING EQUIPMENT

Accurate measuring is important when planning the final position of a stencil. You may need to mark up a wall, box lid or greetings card with registration marks – and when drawing up the stencil itself. Set squares (triangles) give accurate corners and right angles and a metal ruler has a dual role, for measuring and as a straight edge to guide the knife when cutting straight lines within a stencil. Graph paper can be used for planning more formal designs and enlarging a template if you do not have access to a photocopier.

A retractable tape measure is essential for marking up a wall scheme or other large surface, but a dressmaker's measure will do for smaller areas. Light pencil marks and guidelines on wood, walls or paper can easily be removed with an eraser when the paint is dry. Water-soluble or fading fabric marking pens can be used to mark up fabric.

## TRACING AND TRANSFERRING EQUIPMENT

Traditional orange or yellow stencil card is treated with linseed oil (which gives it its characteristic smell) to make it pliable, easy to cut and waterproof. Use a sheet of carbon paper or tracing paper (and a soft pencil) and a ballpoint pen to copy a design on to the card. If you are using clear or semi-transparent acetate, there is no need to transfer the design before cutting out. Adhesive stencil film

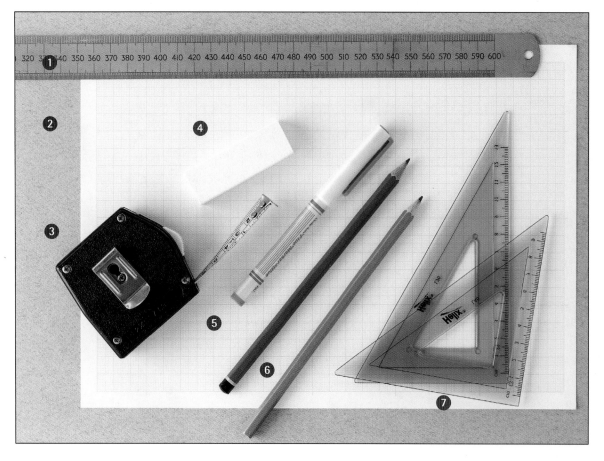

LEFT: Measuring and marking equipment: *1 metal ruler, 2 graph paper, 3 tape measure, 4 eraser, 5 fabric marking pen, 6 pencils, 7 set squares.*

*RIGHT:* Tracing and transferring equipment: 1 *adhesive stencil film,* 2 *stencil card,* 3 *acetate,* 4 *carbon paper,* 5 *tracing paper,* 6 *hard pencil,* 7 *soft pencil,* 8 *ballpoint pen.*

used for airbrushing and other graphic work is ideal for intricate one-off stencils on glass or ceramic surfaces. The design can simply be traced through it with a sharp hard pencil.

## FIXING AND CUTTING EQUIPMENT

If you only intend to make one or two stencils you can cut them on to a piece of thick card (stock), but this tends to blunt any knife quite quickly. Alternatively, a durable self-healing cutting mat will prove invaluable, as it protects the blade and is much safer. If you need extra stability, fix your tracing paper or acetate on to the mat with low-tack masking tape, which will not damage either surface, and a coating of spray mount, which is a light adhesive that can easily be repositioned and does not leave any residue.

When cutting out, you should always work with a sharp blade, which will give a cleaner line and is easier to use. Choose a snap-off knife, which has a supply of new tips, or a craft knife into which new blades can be fitted. A heat knife melts quickly through plastic and speeds up the process: always place a sheet of glass over the design being traced.

*RIGHT:* Fixing and cutting equipment: *1 self-healing cutting mat, 2 spray mount, 3 heat knife, 4 low-tack masking tape, 5 snap-off knife, 6 craft knife.*

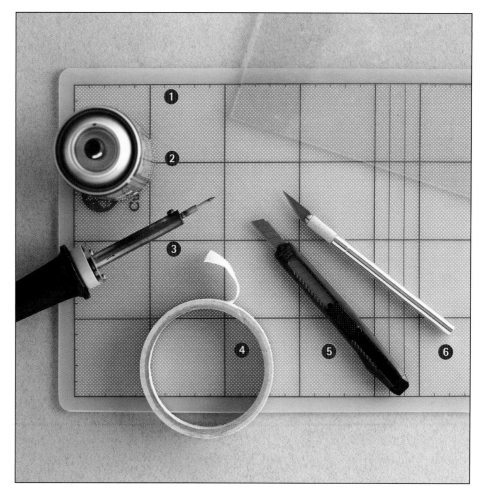

# BRUSHES AND PAINTS

There are various different methods of applying colour to a stencil and many different types of paint that can be used. Small pots of creamy oil-based colour and oil crayons are specially made for use with stencils, but water-based acrylics are easy to use and can be bought from any good art or craft supplier. Special stencil brushes are, however, an essential purchase and the initial outlay of buying a range of several different sizes will prove worthwhile. With care, they will last for years.

## BRUSHES

Stencil brushes are short-handled and their round flat heads are densely packed with firm bristles to let you control the flow of paint. Sizes range from about 5mm to 4cm/¼in to 1½in. Smaller brushes are intended for detailed areas and big ones will cover large areas very quickly. Some have short, stiff bristles for stippling and others are slightly longer and more flexible for a softer, swirled effect. It is worth investing in a good set of stencil brushes. Do not let your brushes or sponges dry out or they will be ruined. It is important to keep your equipment in good condition.

Decorator's brushes are for painting in backgrounds and colour washes. Choose a size to suit your needs. Artist's brushes are used for adding fine details. A sponge roller is another quick way to apply flat colour, while a natural sea sponge, which is better than an artificial one, will produce interesting textures.

*RIGHT:* Brushes and paints: *1 Stencil brushes in different sizes, 2 decorator's brushes, 3 fine artist's brushes, 4 sponge roller, 5 natural sea sponge, 6 artist's acrylic paint, 7 emulsion (latex) paints, 8 spray paint, 9 fabric medium, 10 paint tray, 11 emulsion (latex) paint swatches.*

## PAINTS

Emulsion (latex) paint is used for painting plastered or paper-covered walls. Sample pots (in the same colour range as the room scheme) are a good source of historic and unusual colours for stencilling. Artist's acrylic paint comes in tubes and acrylic craft paint in pots. The latter is very versatile and can be mixed with fabric medium for use on textiles or texture gels to give a variety of three-dimensional effects. Glass and ceramic paints can be used for stencilling, but have to be baked in a hot oven to fix the colour.

Spray paint is fast and easy, and any aerosol from car colour to granite-effect craft spray can be used for stencils. A paint tray or ceramic palette will keep colours separate and is useful for mixing shades with a brush, but a saucer or tile serves the same purpose and is more useful for sponging.

# HOW TO MAKE A STENCIL

A stencil is a negative image of a finished design. The basic shapes that form the image are cut from stencil card or acetate and the links that are left between the spaces are called "ties".

## CARD STENCILS

Stencil card – lightly oiled Manila board – is strong and durable. It is particularly useful if you are going to repeat a design many times. Plastic stencil film is less long-lasting but quicker to use and easy to cut.

It also saves time when working on multi-layered or continuous designs. Using a heat knife (a pointed tool, which melts through the plastic) will speed up the stencil-making process even further.

### Using tracing paper

When transferring a design with tracing paper use this method for an actual-size template. Fix tracing paper over the design with low-tack masking tape, then draw over the outlines using a sharp pencil. Remove the tape and turn the paper over. Rub the back of the lines with a soft pencil. Turn the paper and tape it centrally to a piece of stencil card, then redraw the shapes with a ballpoint pen.

### Using carbon paper

When transferring a design with carbon paper, enlarge or reduce the template to the required size on a scanner or a photocopier. Place the copy centrally on the stencil board and slip a piece of carbon paper, face down, underneath. Tape the edges securely to the stencil board with low-tack masking tape. Draw carefully around each outline with a ballpoint pen, pressing firmly but smoothly.

### Cutting out

Tape the stencil card securely to a self-healing cutting mat or a piece of thick card (stock) with low-tack masking tape. Using a sharp-bladed craft knife, cut along each line at a time within the shapes. It is much easier to start with the largest elements of the stencil, then tackle the more detailed, intricate areas. Always cut towards yourself turning the board with your free hand as necessary, but with care, to create smooth curves. Don't worry if you slice through a tie (one of the card "bridges" that link the cut out shapes): they are easily repaired with adhesive tape.

## PLASTIC STENCILS

The benefit of using plastic stencils such as acetate is that you do not have to transfer the design but can cut the shape out directly.

### Preparing to cut

Place a sheet of glass (tape the edges if they are rough) over the page of the book or photocopy you have chosen. Cut a piece of plastic at least 5cm/2in larger all round than the design and tape it to the glass with low-tack masking tape. Peel this off carefully when the stencil is complete. For extra security, you can lightly spray the back with spray mount.

### Using a craft knife

Always use a sharp craft knife to cut around each element within the design as for a card stencil, but take extra care because the blade is more liable to slip on the smooth surface of the glass than it is on card. Remove the tape, lift the design and check that nothing has been missed out. Neaten any rough edges with the knife or a small pair of curved blade scissors.

### Using a heat knife

When cutting out with a knife, read the manufacturer's instructions carefully before starting and practise on an offcut or spare piece of acetate to get the hang of using the knife before you start. Always use a sharp blade to give a cleaner line and make sure the blade is secure. Trace the point of the knife steadily around each outline, without pressing too hard and keeping an even pressure. If you work too slowly the line will be too wide so trace each element smoothly in a single motion.

# APPLYING COLOUR

There are several different ways of colouring in a stencil with acrylic paints, using a brush, sponge or foam roller, each of which produces its own individual look. Take inspiration from the suggestions shown here, then go on to create your own special effects to suit your own ideas.

## BRUSH EFFECTS

A single stencil can be used in many ways by applying paint in different colours and textures. The examples on the next few pages show you how to create just some of the many possible paint effects. Experiment and try them out before you start work on an actual project. Start off by securing the stencil to the surface being decorated with masking tape (use the low-tack version which will not damage the background) or spray mount. This adhesive keeps the whole stencil flat, reducing the risk of paint seeping under the edges, but should only be used in a well-ventilated space. Wipe the stencil clean of paint and glue when you have finished working. An acetate stencil can be washed in soapy water and dried on kitchen paper.

### Using a stencil brush

Dip the flat tip of the stencil brush into a saucer of paint, then remove the surplus by rubbing the bristles on to kitchen paper in a circular motion. Avoid overloading: it is better to apply two light coats of paint rather than one heavy one. Always wash the bristles in warm soapy water when the paint builds up and when changing colours – a quick blast from a hairdryer will speed up the drying process.

### Blocked colour

Always hold the brush lightly at right angles when stencilling, so that the paint will not get underneath the stencil itself and smudge the outline. Load the brush and dab it up and down within the stencil. You should be making a tapping movement rather than sweeping the brush as when painting. Build up the paint gradually to produce a solid block of colour and wait until it is dry before removing the stencil.

### Stippled colour

This technique can be used to create differently shaded elements within a stencil to give the finished design an almost three-dimensional appearance. Block the colour as above for the darkest parts (around the outer edge of the petals in this example) and apply the same colour much more sparsely to the lighter areas. Take time to build up layers of colour and rework the stencil until you are pleased with the result.

## Using more than one colour

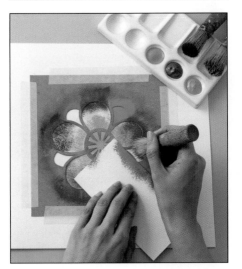

If you are using two or more colours on a stencil, it is important to use just one paint at a time, changing or washing the brushes in between use to keep the elements distinct and the colours clean. If the different coloured sections are adjacent, use strips of low-tack masking tape or a piece of paper to protect the areas that are not being painted.

## Multicoloured stippling

It is possible to create a huge range of textures and great depth of colour by applying several colours to a stencil. Here the outside edges of the petals have been stippled in solid pink, which fades through to a soft orange. In contrast, the star-shaped flower centre is more solid and the dense colour of the leaves is broken up with pink stippling.

## Dry brushing

As its name suggests, this paint effect uses only a very small amount of paint. Load the stencil brush, then wipe most of the paint off on to kitchen paper. Fill in the shapes with light, straight strokes, allowing a little of the background colour to show through as you apply each successive layer. Here, all the strokes have been made from the centre outwards.

## Using a sponge

Sponging is a good way to fill a large or small stencil with interesting texture. You can use a synthetic household sponge for dense colour, but natural sponges give a more open and varied effect. Dip the sponge into the paint, remove the excess by dabbing it on to newspaper or kitchen towel then dab it lightly over the stencil.

## Using a roller

Sponge rollers can be used to apply a coat of a single colour or, as here, to produce subtly blended effects. Put a blob of each paint in a saucer, in a short line. Push the dry roller over the paint and roll it backwards and forwards until the edges are blurred, then roll it over the stencil.

## Stippling from the edges

Using a very dry stencil brush (dab most of the paint off the bristles before you start), stipple from the outside of the design, working inwards. By the time you get to the centre, there should be hardly any paint left on your brush, ensuring a very soft paint effect in this area.

## PAINT EFFECTS

A stencil brush, versatile as it may be, is not the only way to apply paint through a stencil. Sponging and rolling are both very quick and effective alternative techniques, particularly if you are going to repeat the design across a large area, such as a wall. As with brush effects, it is a good idea to have several sponges or brushes to hand when working on a stencil that uses more than one colour. Pour a small amount of each paint into a separate saucer so that the colours do not become mixed.

### Sponge effect

The open texture of a natural sponge makes it ideal for building up layers of colour. The holes within it produce round or oval spaces within the paint surface, which means that the previous layers are still visible. Try not to cover the background completely as a few white speckles make the finished design look bright and lively.

### Sponge roller effect

Sponge rollers – cylinders of sponge fixed on to a plastic handle – come in widths from 2.5cm/1in up to 15cm/6in. Use narrow ones for details and wider ones for applying a first coat to the stencil or covering bigger spaces. When working on a multicoloured design, mask off the areas that are not to be painted, because the roller is not as precise as a brush.

### Adding a drop shadow

A drop shadow is a deceptively simple way of giving a sophisticated feeling of depth to a flat motif. Decide where the finished design is to go, then position the stencil slightly below and to the right of that position. Stipple the right-hand side of the design lightly in grey paint. When dry, stencil the main design above and to the left of the shadow.

### Adding texture

There are several different texture gels available from good craft stores, all designed for use with artist's acrylic paints. The gels range from ground pumice stone to very small plastic balls, or metallic glitter. They are stirred into the paint, which is then stippled thickly on to the stencil. A simple do-it-yourself grainy texture can, however, easily be produced by adding grains of sand to acrylic paint or using powdered multipurpose filler.

## SPECIAL PAINTS

Several of the projects in this book use artist's acrylic paint, which has many advantages. It is relatively cheap and economic to use, readily available, and it comes in a wide spectrum of colours and can be mixed to create myriad others. It also dries quickly and can be washed from brushes, rollers or sponges with warm, soapy water. There are, of course, many alternatives, each of which has its own individual character and purpose. Some of them are illustrated here and once you have tried them, search the shelves of your local art store and experiment with glitter paints, wax crayons, oil sticks, translucent glass paints or watercolours.

### Using spray paint

When using an aerosol it is important that you mask off the surrounding area completely with sheets of newspaper. However carefully you spray the paint, small particles inevitably hover in the air and will mark any background that has not been covered. You should also work in a well-ventilated room or outdoors.

### Spray paint effects

Mask off with card or masking tape all the parts of the stencil that are not being used before applying the first colour. Press the button and move the can across the surface a few times. Build up several thin layers of paint, rather than one thick one, which will form a pool and seep under the edges of the stencil.

### Fabric paint

Wash and press the fabric or garment before stencilling to remove any residue from the manufacturing process. Tape a length of spare fabric on to a pad of newspaper (to absorb any excess paint that goes through the fabric), or insert a piece of card (stock) inside a garment to protect the back. Once it is dry, heat-fix the paint according to the manufacturer's instructions.

### Ceramic paint

Adhesive stencil film, used by graphic artists, is very useful when painting on glass or ceramic surfaces. Trace the design in pencil, then remove the backing and stick the film to a clean surface. Use a sharp craft knife to cut out the shapes, and apply the paint sparingly with a brush, sponge or roller. The finished object should then be fired by baking it in the oven, as instructed by the manufacturer.

### Metallic wax

This creamy wax, used by gilders and picture framers, comes in a range of metallic shades from pale platinum and gold through to bronze and pewter. Apply it by wrapping your forefinger in a piece of soft cloth and rubbing your fingertip over the surface of the wax. Transfer it to the stencil by rubbing in small circles until the surface appears burnished. More than one colour can be applied for a luxurious effect: apply the lightest shade first.

# REGISTRATION MARKS

If a stencil has more than one component, the two parts must line up exactly. This is easy with acetate stencils, as the first layer of paint will be visible. It is more difficult with card stencils, so registration marks – small crosses or notches – cut into both stencils in the same position are used. They are transferred by pencil and the overlay is positioned so that the lines show through the second set of registration marks. Use them also for a repeated border where the motifs overlap to create the finished design.

## BORDERS AND TWO-LAYERED STENCILS

Elegant stencilled borders provide the finishing touch in a room. They are ideal for creating "frames" and panel effects. Use them to define space, such as a dado (chair) rail or to create a painted border around a floor.

### Using a card stencil for a border

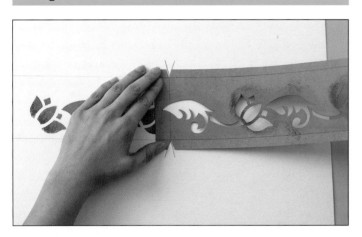

Each repeated motif should be positioned at the same level. Once you have transferred the stencil on to card, draw a line along the bottom edge of the design, continuing it out to the left and right edges. Draw a line and match the two up for each repeat. Transfer the registration marks at the beginning and end of each repeat on to the card and cut notches at these points. Transfer the second notch on to the surface with a pencil "V" and match the first notch up to this point each time the stencil is used.

### Using acetate for a border

Clear sheets of acetate are much easier to use than card when stencilling borders. You can line them up by eye, rather than by using registration marks. It is still, however, important to draw a baseline on to the surface so that the stencil will be straight and horizontal. For two-layered stencils, the design can be lined up by eye. You can also transfer the registration marks with a waterproof pen and make small slits along them. Pencil a cross within these marks when the first layer has been finished and match the second stencil to them.

### Two-layered stencils

When transferring the two elements that make up the design on to stencil card, draw in the cross-shaped registration marks. Carefully cut out each stencil, then rule in pencil lines to join up the four crosses, making a rectangle or square. Snip out the corners to make right-angled notches. Before removing the first stencil, make a two-sided pencil mark like an arrow tip along each corner. Position the second stencil within these marks and it will then be aligned precisely to the first.

# ONE-OFF AND REVERSE STENCILS

Stencil-making does not always have to be time-consuming and formal, nor does it require specialist equipment. These one-off techniques show that stencilled decoration can also be spontaneous and unstructured. Use them for stationery or paper projects such as greetings cards or wrapping paper, or let your imagination run wild and stencil lacy patterns on to a silk scarf or a flurry of leaf outlines across a wall. Instead of starting with a negative image, as with a regular stencil, reverse stencils are in fact positive images, with outlines defined by the paint. Found natural objects, such as ferns or dried, pressed leaves, are a good source of unexpected shapes, or try using lace or paper doilies.

## Using leaves

Collect a selection of interestingly shaped autumn leaves and press them under a heavy book overnight. To use them as stencils, hold the leaf down with the fingers of one hand or fix to the surface with a reusable putty adhesive and block in colour around the edge, using a wide brush loaded with paint.

## Using lace

Use a brush or aerosol spray paint to transfer the intricate designs of woven lace without distorting the fabric. Fix the lace on to the surface to be decorated with spray mount and mask off the surrounding area. Spray two or more light coats of paint across the surface, using even strokes, until the pattern is well defined.

## Paper cuts

Simple, symmetrical designs that are going to be used just once can be cut from thin coloured paper. Fold the paper in half vertically and draw one side of a heart along the crease with a pencil. Cut out the shape with sharp scissors and flatten out the paper, then stencil as usual. Once you have mastered this quick and versatile technique, you could go on to make more complex designs, such as paper snowflakes, Christmas trees, or chains of little figures.

# VARIATIONS ON A THEME

The stencils that appear in this book have each been designed with a specific project in mind – a complex wall treatment, a kitchen curtain, a cushion or a simple greetings card. All of them, however, can be altered and reinterpreted endlessly. There are many ways in which you can vary colour schemes, invert or reverse the motif, change the spacing, enlarge or reduce the design, or print it on an unexpected surface. Here are some ideas for creating different layouts and patterns. Use a little imagination, and you will be able to come up with countless variations of your own.

## Positive and negative images

The negative image on the left – a pale flower branch in a single colour on a very dark green background – is a graphic design. It is, in fact, exactly the same design as the delicate spray on the right – a positive image that has been stencilled more conventionally in colour on white paper. Light-on-dark images always have strong visual impact. Try stencilling a white pattern on a pastel background for a more subtle, but still unusual look.

## Mirror image

Any stencil design that is not symmetrical can be flipped over to create its mirror image. Paint the first motif as usual. Clean off any surplus paint from the stencil and leave it to dry. Turn it over, line up the stencil carefully opposite the first motif, and block in the second motif. This is a good way to create a simple border, by stencilling pairs of reversed motifs above a dado (chair) rail or below a ceiling coving (cove molding).

## Repeating around a point

This pattern, in which a roughly square design has been repeated four times around a centre point, is reminiscent of a tiled wall. It can be copied with any symmetrical stencil. Draw two lines that intersect at right angles, then two more at 45 degrees to the first pair. Mark the base of the first motif, close to the centre point, then line the stencil up along the diagonal line. Stencil three more motifs on the diagonals, ensuring that they all start at the same distance along the lines.

## Random repeats

A small, self-contained motif like this butterfly or a floral motif can be repeated at random across the surface. Use a single colour, or stencil each one in a different shade to produce a lively, interesting pattern, which would work equally well on a wall or on fabric.

## Changing sizes

This pattern uses a pretty Japanese flower, which has been enlarged to make a bigger stencil. The combination of the two sizes gives vitality to the design, and shows just how many different ways there are of using a very simple motif to produce a sophisticated result.

## Rotating with blocked leaves

Using a very dry brush with a tiny amount of paint, rotate the bristles in a circular motion. This rotating action leaves enough paint on the surface for a lighter, softer look than a block application. Use the same effect in a darker colour on the inside of the petals.

## Rotating and soft shading

Using a very dry brush with a tiny amount of paint, place your brush on one side of the stencil and rotate the brush in small circles. Repeat this action, using a slightly darker colour on the edges of the stencil, to create the effect of soft shading.

## Rotating and shading in two colours

This is a similar effect to rotating and soft shading, but is more directional. Using a very dry brush with a tiny amount of paint, place your brush in the centre of the flower and rotate the bristles slightly outwards. Repeat this action, using a slightly darker colour.

## HALF-DROP REPEATS

A regular repeated design looks very effective on a large expanse of wall, giving the illusion of a printed wallpaper pattern. Stencil a few motifs roughly on to sheets of paper, cut them out and tape them to the wall before you begin, to get an idea of the finished look.

The framework for the pattern should be measured up very carefully, especially in older houses where walls and windows may not be perfectly straight. Start by marking a vertical line down the left edge of the wall using chalked builder's string and bear in mind any fixed architectural features such as light fittings, chimney breasts (fireplace projections), architraves (trims), alcoves and corners that you will need to work around.

1 To mark up the wall, decide how far apart the motifs are to lie, horizontally and vertically. Cut a rectangle of card (stock) to these measurements and draw two lines to divide it into quarters. Cut a notch at each end of the lines. Use the card as a guide to draw a light pencil grid across the wall.

2 To stencil a half-drop repeat: in the same way, draw two lines across the stencil and notch the ends. Use these marks to match the stencil to the grid. Stencil in the first horizontal row of motifs, then position the next row in the spaces below. Continue until the wall is covered.

3 To make half-drop repeats on fabric, mark a grid on to fabric, decide how far apart the motifs are to be, then fold and press lightly along these lines. When the fabric is opened out these lines will appear as creases, which will disappear when the fabric is pressed once again.

# PREPARING AND FINISHING

As with any home decorating project, whether it is painting an old wooden chair or putting a new paint effect on a wall, time invested in preparation pays off by giving you a professional result at the end. Don't be in too much of a hurry to start, plan carefully and work in an orderly way. Collect together all the equipment and tools you will need, including the cleaning materials for tidying up afterwards and a stack of old newspaper to protect the floor or work surface. An overall or smock will protect your clothes.

## PREPARING WALLS

If you are working on a freshly plastered wall, make sure that it is completely dry before painting it with emulsion (latex) paint in your desired base colour. However clean they appear, previously decorated surfaces should always be washed down well with detergent or sugar soap to remove accumulated dust and grease. If you wish your stencils to have a more textured background than that which is given by flat emulsion paint, try using one of these simple paint effects on the wall.

Most modern acrylic paints are tough and waterproof, but your finished stencils may need to be sealed, especially in humid areas such as kitchens and bathrooms, or if they are in rooms which receive lots of wear and tear such as hallways and landings. Leave the painted surface to dry thoroughly for a week, then seal with matt (flat) varnish.

## PREPARING WOOD

New or unprimed wood should be sanded down with medium- and then fine-grade abrasive paper. When the surface is smooth, wipe it over with a damp cloth to remove any residual dust and leave to dry. If you wish to darken the natural colour, use a wood stain, diluting it with water for a lighter shade and painting it in long strokes along the grain. Otherwise, prepare with a clear wood sealer. Water-based sealants are easier to use and do not have the yellowish hue of their oil-based equivalents. When the stencilling is complete, apply two coats of water-based varnish to give a hardwearing finish to the wood.

### Colour washing

This can be done with a light paint on a darker background or vice versa, or for a more subtle look with two very closely toning colours. Dilute the second coat with water, adding more water for a lighter colour, then paint it on the wall using loose brushstrokes painted in one or many directions, or use a wide roller.

### Sponging

Using a natural sea sponge creates an open texture and is a quick way to cover a large surface. Wash and rinse the sponge, then squeeze out the excess moisture. Dip it into a saucer of diluted emulsion (latex) paint then dab it on to the wall in a circular pattern or straight lines, depending on the effect required.

*ABOVE: Always sand new or unprimed wood before stencilling to create a key.*

# THE PROJECTS

Stencilling is a quick and effective way to revive an old piece of furniture or flea-market find, or to add decoration to a plain flat-pack chest of drawers or table. Here you'll find a selection of over 30 wonderful projects that you can make for your home or give as a gift to mark a birthday or other special occasion. There are ideas for furniture, soft furnishings and home accessories, including a flamboyant Hawaiian Hibiscus Cabinet, an elegant Garden Shadows Blind, and a tropical Citrus Fruit Tray.

*ABOVE: Old-fashioned style trains and carriages are popular themes for children's rooms and storage.*

*LEFT: Graphic rose print cushions add elegance to a light, modern living room or conservatory.*

# BRONZE CHAIR

This handsome gilded design was inspired by the high-quality "Hitchcock" chairs popular in America in the 19th century, named after the man who mass-produced them. The brilliance of the colour comes from real bronze powder (or gold powder, which is more expensive), and the effect is quite different to bronze or gold paint, or bronze or gold leaf. The original makers used the finest velvet to apply the powder, moulding the shapes of fruit and flowers by varying the amount of powder.

1 Rub down any existing paintwork with abrasive paper.

2 Dust off the surface with a clean cotton rag.

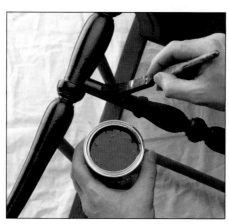

3 Paint the chair with black emulsion (latex) paint.

*OPPOSITE: The stencil for this chair is very intricate and will take time to cut out.*

4 Photocopy the stencil pattern at the back of the book, enlarging it to fit your chair back. Spray the back of the pattern with spray mount and stick it on to stencil card. Cut out the small shapes using a craft knife and cutting mat.

5 Complete cutting out the pattern, then cut away the extra card so that the stencil fits your chair back. Lay the stencil in position on the chair back.

6 Place a small amount of size on a plate. Using a stencil brush, stipple the size through the shapes. Use the size sparingly, but fill in each shape.

7 When the size is just tacky (see manufacturer's instructions), dust on bronze or gold powder. Work it into the size by applying it with a piece of lint or velvet.

8 Leave the bronze or gold powder for 1–2 hours to set. Gently wipe away any excess with a small square of lint or soft velvet.

9 Highlight details on the rest of the chair. Apply size with a fine artist's brush, then add the bronze or gold powder. If desired, you can soften the gold effect with a coat of antiquing varnish, which will also protect the stencilling. Clear satin varnish will give protection without dulling the gold.

# SCANDINAVIAN CHAIR

These motifs can be adjusted to fit any style of wooden chair, which can be decorated as simply or lavishly as you wish. Here, white paint is applied to a blue chair but other combinations such as red paint on a white chair would also look good.

1 Trace the templates at the back of the book. Place a piece of carbon paper face down on to a sheet of stencil card. Tape the tracings on top. Re-draw the templates with a sharp pencil to transfer the design. Using a sharp-bladed craft knife and cutting mat cut out the stencils, cutting straight lines against a metal ruler.

2 Tape the large star flower stencil centrally on to the chair seat. Using a flat paintbrush, spread a thin coat of white paint on to a ceramic tile. Dab at the paint with a stencil brush and stencil the flower motif. Leave to dry completely. Apply a second coat of paint for a stronger image then remove the stencil.

3 Tape the tulip stencil upright to the centre of the upper rail of the chair. Lightly stencil the motif with the white acrylic paint. Leave to dry then remove the stencil.

 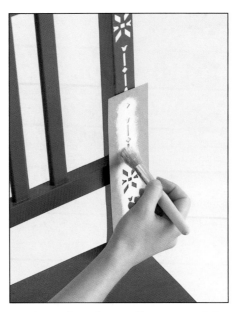 

4 Stencil the tulip again at each end of the rail. Stencil a medium star flower between the tulips. If your chair does not have enough space for a medium star flower, stencil one of the smaller images instead.

5 Tape the strip stencil to one upright of the back on the chair, placing the single diamond at the centre. Shorten the stencil to fit if necessary. Stencil the upright. Leave it to dry completely then swivel the stencil, matching the single diamond position to stencil the other half of the upright.

6 Repeat this process on the other chair upright. Stencil the front and sides of the legs in the same way. Shorten the stencil or repeat the images to fit the length of your chair legs.

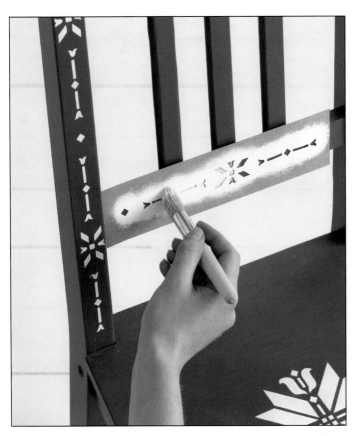 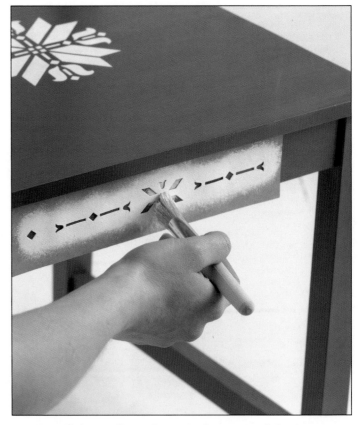

7 Tape the strip stencil to the lower rail, placing the small star flower at the centre. Shorten the stencil to fit if necessary. Stencil the rail.

8 Stencil the small star flower in the centre of the front seat support. Stencil any other parts of the chair using the entire strip stencil or just a section of it.

# PAINTED DRAWERS

Jazz up plain drawers with bright paintbox colours and simple daisy stencils. The stencils could also be used to decorate larger pieces of furniture such as a chest of drawers for a child's room or kitchen units. Sample pots of emulsion (latex) paint are ideal to use on small projects.

## You will need

- set of wooden drawers
- fine-grade abrasive paper
- emulsion (latex) paints in various bright colours
- medium and small decorator's paintbrushes
- screwdriver
- acetate sheet
- craft knife and self-healing cutting mat
- stencil brushes
- matt (flat) acrylic varnish
- wood glue (optional)

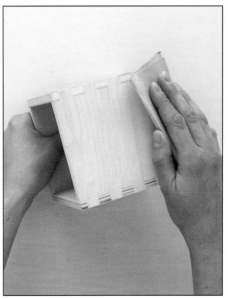

1 Remove the drawers and sand down the frame and drawers to remove any rough areas or patches of old paint.

2 Paint the drawer frame with emulsion (latex) paint. Leave to dry, then apply a second coat of paint.

3 Unscrew the drawer knobs and paint each drawer in a different-coloured emulsion paint. Leave to dry and apply a second coat. Trace the flower template at the back of the book and cut a stencil from acetate sheet using a craft knife and cutting mat.

OPPOSITE: *If you use more muted colours such as pale green or cream, you can create a much subtler effect.*

4 When the drawers are dry, position the flower stencil in the centre of a drawer and, using a stencil brush and paint in a contrasting colour, stencil on the flower. Leave to dry.

5 Stencil a daisy flower in the centre of each drawer, using a different colour paint for each one.

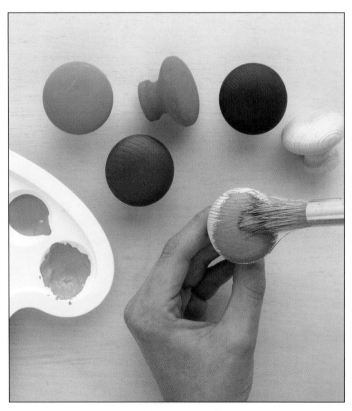

6 Paint the drawer knobs with two coats of paint, leaving them to dry between coats. Leave to dry.

7 Screw or glue a painted knob to the centre of each drawer. Varnish the drawers with matt acrylic varnish. Leave to dry before reassembling.

# TRAIN TOY BOX

This chugging train stencil will fit any child's toy box. Simply add or decrease the number of wagons to suit your requirements. You could add more wagons to extend the train around the entire box.

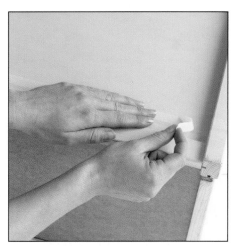

1 Stick a length of masking tape around the toy box immediately below the intended position of the rails. Stick another length of tape 5mm/¼in above the first. Keep the tape parallel with the base of the toy box.

2 Using a flat paintbrush, spread a thin coat of grey paint on to a ceramic tile. Dab at the paint with a stencil brush and stencil the rails. Leave the paint to dry then carefully pull off the tape.

3 Trace the toy box and clouds templates at the back of the book. Tape a piece of acetate to the tracings. Using a craft knife and cutting mat cut out the stencils, cutting straight lines against a metal ruler. You will need two toy box stencils – the train engine, wagons and smoke, then the wheels and the details. Also cut out the registration marks to help guide your positioning.

4 Tape the engine, wagons and smoke stencil to the front of the box, placing the lower registration marks on the upper edge of the rails. Mark the top registration marks and the top strut of the lower registration marks with a soft pencil. Using the flat paintbrush, spread a thin coat of red paint on to the tile. Dab at the paint with a stencil brush and stencil the engine. Leave to dry.

5 Using the flat paintbrush, spread a thin coat of aquamarine and pink paint on to the tile. Stencil the wagons with the aquamarine and pink paint. Spread grey and white paint on to the tile. Dab at one paint then the other and stencil the steam to create a mottled effect. Leave to dry completely then remove the stencil.

6 Tape the wheels and details stencil in place, matching the registration marks. Stencil the chimneys using yellow paint. Stencil the wheels and couplings with blue paint. Stencil the coal with black paint. Hold the stencil brush upright when stencilling and move the brush in a circular motion. Leave to dry. Remove the stencil.

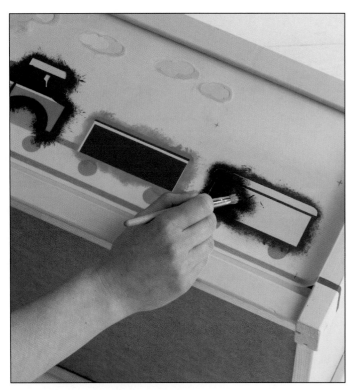

7 Move the wagon stencil along the box, matching the right-hand registration marks of the previous wagon with the left-hand registration marks of the next. Stencil the wheels and couplings with blue paint. Leave to dry. Replace the stencil with a wagon stencil, matching the registration marks. Stencil the wagon with purple paint.

8 Leave to dry then erase the registration marks. Tape the clouds stencil centrally to the lid of the box. Use the flat paintbrush to spread a thin coat of white paint on to the tile. Stencil the clouds with the white paint. Leave to dry. To make the toy box hard-wearing paint it with two or three coats of clear matt (flat) varnish.

# HAWAIIAN HIBISCUS CABINET

Transform a plain wooden cabinet with this flamboyant floral stencil. Enlarge the template on a photocopier to fit your cupboard door.

1 If necessary, fill any screwholes in the cabinet with wood filler. Leave to dry, then sand lightly with abrasive paper. Paint the cabinet with apricot emulsion (latex) paint. Leave to dry, then sand lightly with abrasive paper. Wipe with a damp rag. Apply a second coat of paint.

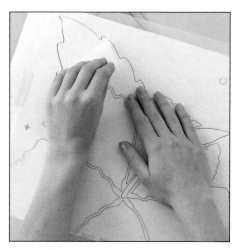

2 Enlarge the template at the back of the book on a photocopier. Tape a piece of acetate to the photocopy with masking tape. Resting on a cutting mat, cut out the stencils with a craft knife. You will need three stencils – the petals, the stigma and leaves, and the stamens and spots.

3 Stick the petals stencil to the door with spray mount. Mark the registration marks with a soft pencil. Using a flat paintbrush, spread a thin coat of pink paint on to a ceramic tile. Dab at the paint with a stencil brush and stencil the petals.

4 Leave to dry. Shade the petals at the centre of the flower with apricot acrylic paint. Leave to dry then remove the stencil.

5 Stick the stigma and leaves stencil in place with spray mount, matching the registration marks. Stencil the stigma with apricot paint.

6 Stencil the leaves with lime green paint. Leave to dry.

7 Shade the leaves along their centres and around the petals with mid-green paint to darken the areas and give a slight three-dimensional effect.

8 Leave to dry then remove the stencil. Stick the stamens and spots stencil to the door with spray mount, matching the registration marks. Mix a little lime green and yellow paint and use to stencil the stamens.

9 Stencil the spots with the mixed lime green and yellow paint. Leave to dry.

10 Shade the edges of the spots with apricot paint. Remove the stencil and erase the registration marks.

11 Position part of the spots stencil on the side of the cabinet. Tape in place and stencil the spots with the mixed lime green and yellow paint. Leave to dry. Move the stencil along to stencil another part of the side if necessary. Repeat on the other side of the cabinet and on the top if that will be visible.

12 Set the cabinet aside to dry overnight then remove the stencil. Apply two coats of clear matt varnish, lightly sanding the cabinet between coats. This will protect the cabinet from wear and tear.

*OPPOSITE: Any large single flower can be used to decorate a cabinet.*

# CELTIC KNOT BOX

Intertwined, maze-like designs like this circular motif appeared on Irish carvings and manuscripts as early as the fifth century AD. The knot is made up of four quarters, repeated individually in the corners of the box.

### You will need

- medium-grade abrasive paper
- wooden box
- wood filler (optional)
- acrylic primer
- medium decorator's paintbrush
- acrylic paints in pale and dark gold
- tracing paper and pen or carbon paper and sharp pencil
- masking tape
- stencil card
- craft knife and self-healing cutting mat
- ruler
- soft pencil
- spray mount
- stencil brush
- green stencil paint
- aerosol matt (flat) or gloss varnish

1 Sand down the box to key the surface and, if necessary, fill in any holes or deep scratches with wood filler.

2 Paint the box with a coat of white wood primer to prepare the surface. Porous wood may need two coats.

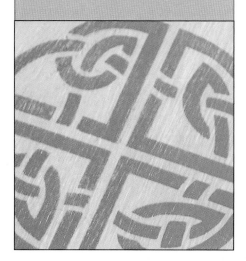

3 Paint the box with one or two layers of pale gold paint.

4 To give interest to the pale yellow surface of the box, colour wash it with dark gold paint. Dilute the paint with four parts of water and apply with broad strokes using a decorator's brush.

5 Trace the template at the back of the book. Tape it on to stencil card and cut out, using a craft knife and cutting mat. Mark the quarter sections on the stencil. Using a soft pencil, lightly pencil in two lines to divide the box top into quarters. Spray the stencil with spray mount, then line it up along the pencil lines and fill in with green paint.

6 Stencil in a quarter section of the knot in each corner of the box. Line it up so that the centre division of the stencil lies at the edge of the lid and mask off carefully with tape.

7 Stencil the bottom of each side of the box in the same way using sections of the main motif that will fit neatly into the right-angled corners. Mask off the surrounding area as necessary.

8 Once the paint is quite dry, sand the box lightly to give it a distressed finish. Spray with one or more coats of craft varnish to protect the surface with a matt (flat) or gloss finish.

# DAISY STOOL

Give a simple wooden stool a new lease of life with pretty folk art motifs. The fine stripes around the legs are achieved by stencilling between strips of masking tape.

1 Trace the templates at the back of the book. Tape a piece of acetate to the tracings. Using a craft knife and cutting mat, cut out the stencils. You will need two stencils for each seat flower – the circle and leaves, then the flower centre, petals, stalk and leaf veins. Remember to cut out the registration marks.

2 Measure the seat and divide it into quarters with a soft pencil. Tape the circle and leaves stencils of the seat flowers inside two of the quarters. Mark the registration marks in pencil. Using a flat paintbrush, spread a thin coat of beige paint on to a ceramic tile. Lightly dab at the paint with a stencil brush and stencil the circles and leaves holding the stencil brush upright and moving it in a circular motion. Leave to dry then repeat in the other quarters.

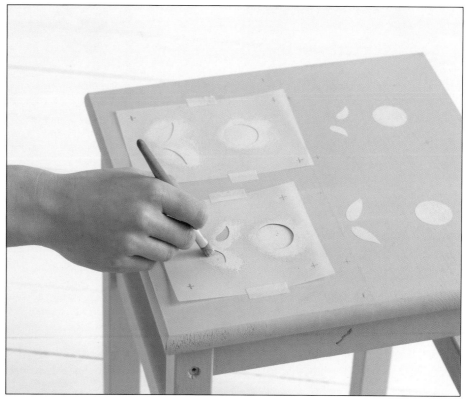

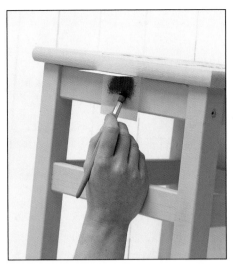

3 When the paint is dry tape the flower centre, petals, stalk and leaf veins stencils in place, matching the registration marks. Stencil the cut-outs with dark green paint. Leave to dry then repeat on the other flowers. Leave to dry then erase the pencil marks.

4 Position the small flower stencil centrally on a top strut of the stool. Carefully stencil the flower with dark green paint, protecting the surrounding area from paint with a piece of card (stock). Repeat the stencil centrally on the other top struts.

5 Tape the pair of leaves of one seat flower stencil centrally to a lower strut. Stencil the leaves with dark green paint. Leave to dry. Remove the stencil and tape the leaf veins stencil in place. Tape over the stem cut-out. Stencil the leaf veins with beige paint. Repeat on the other struts.

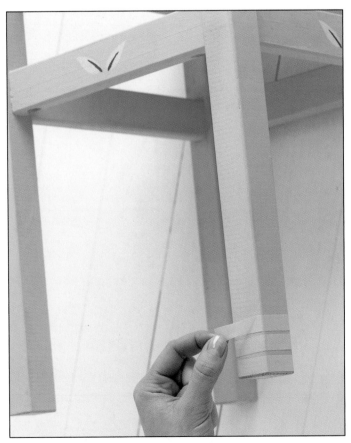

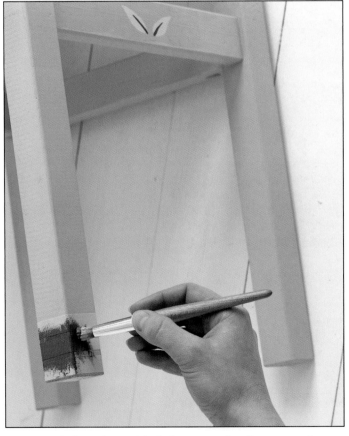

6 Stick three lengths of low-tack masking tape around one stool leg, leaving a 5mm/¼in gap between each tape to create stripes around the bottom of the leg.

7 Stencil the stripes with dark green paint. Repeat on the other legs. Peel off the tape when the paint has dried. Give the stool two coats of varnish to finish.

# TEA TABLE

A fun approach to stencilling using a simple reverse technique that doesn't involve cutting any stencils, this trompe l'oeil table top is quick and easy to do and can transform an old table. The paper doilies give a pretty, lacy effect, complemented by the blue and white polka dot "tablecloth".

1 Sand down the table top, sides and legs to key the surface ready for the new paint. Use medium then fine-grade abrasive paper to give a smooth finish. If you have an electric sanding machine, this will speed up the preparation.

2 Paint the table top with a coat of white primer and leave to dry completely. If you prefer a more subtle paint finish with some of the underlying colour showing through, make this a very light coat.

3 Spray the wrong side of the first doily lightly with spray mount and position it along the centre of one side of the table. Smooth it down gently with the flat of your hand, then fix the other three doilies in place spacing them at regular intervals.

*OPPOSITE: You can vary the pattern of the stencilled doilies to create an individual place setting if you wish.*

4 Using a very small amount of blue paint and a dry stencil brush, block in a circle of colour around the doilies, filling in all the spaces and covering the edge completely.

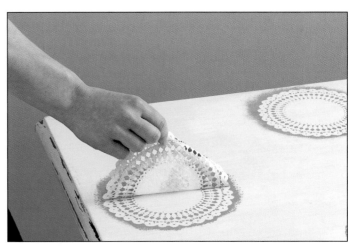

5 When the paint is dry, carefully pull back and discard the doilies. Stencil the other three "mats" in the same way taking care not to overload the brush with paint.

6 Stick the adhesive dots randomly over the remaining white paint, spacing them at roughly equal intervals across the surface of the table top.

7 Using a stippling action and a dry stencil brush, paint over the rest of the table, filling in the space between the stencils with an even layer of colour.

8 Leave to dry completely. Gently lift off each adhesive dot in turn using the sharp point of a craft knife, being careful not to dig it into the wood so you do not scratch the surface of the paint.

9 Paint the rest of the table with blue paint, paying attention to any moulded areas around the top edge and on the legs. When dry, apply two coats of matt (flat) varnish to make the table top hard-wearing.

# AFRICAN BEDSIDE CHEST

**W**arm rustic colours and a bold graphic design have transformed a dull modern chest of drawers. The African motifs are stencilled across a band of subtle colour, which is applied with a natural sponge.

### You will need

- natural sponge
- flat paintbrush
- acrylic paints in yellow ochre and terracotta
- ceramic tile
- chest of drawers, painted cream
- tracing paper and pen
- masking tape
- acetate sheet
- craft knife and self-healing cutting mat
- adhesive spray
- stencil brush
- matt (flat) varnish and brush

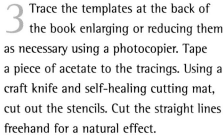

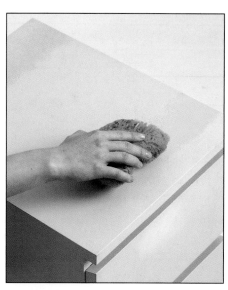

1 Moisten the sponge. Using a flat paintbrush, spread a thin coat of yellow ochre paint on to a ceramic tile. Dab at the paint with the sponge.

2 Dab the paint in a 12cm/4$\frac{1}{2}$in wide band on the top of the chest approximately 4cm/1$\frac{1}{2}$in from the front and back edges. Leave to dry.

3 Trace the templates at the back of the book enlarging or reducing them as necessary using a photocopier. Tape a piece of acetate to the tracings. Using a craft knife and self-healing cutting mat, cut out the stencils. Cut the straight lines freehand for a natural effect.

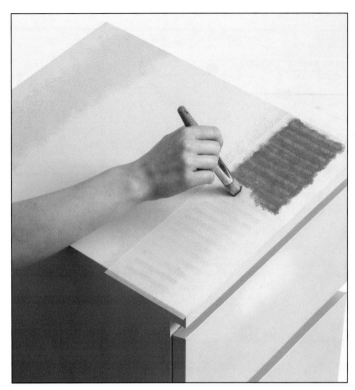

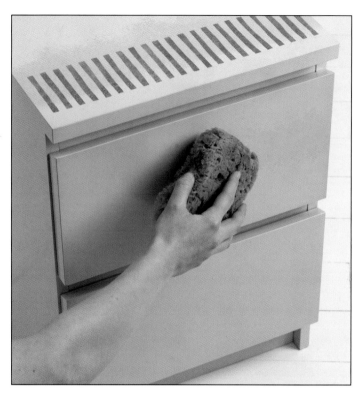

4 Stick the top stencil to the top of the chest at the front with spray mount. Using the flat paintbrush, spread a thin coat of terracotta paint on to the tile. Dab at the paint with a stencil brush and stencil the top of the chest. Move the stencil to the back of the top of the chest and repeat.

5 Using a flat paintbrush, spread a thin coat of yellow ochre acrylic paint on to the ceramic tile. Dab at the paint with a natural sponge. Dab the paint across a drawer front. Leave to dry completely.

6 Stick the zigzag stencil to one half of a drawer front with spray mount. Stencil the zigzags with terracotta paint. Leave to dry then remove the stencil.

7 Stick the rotating lines stencil to the other half of the drawer front with spray mount and stencil with terracotta paint. Leave to dry then remove the stencil. Paint with two or three coats of matt (flat) varnish to protect the chest.

# STRIPED TABLE AND CHAIRS

Pencils, paintbrushes and colourful stripes will provide inspiration for the young artist in your family on this charming set of child-sized furniture.

### You will need

- 12mm/½in wide masking tape
- small wooden table and chairs, painted cream
- set square (triangle)
- craft knife and self-healing cutting mat
- metal ruler
- flat paintbrush
- acrylic paints in pale blue, apricot, aquamarine, lilac and grey
- ceramic tile
- stencil brush
- piece of card (stock)
- tracing paper and pen
- acetate sheet
- soft pencil
- eraser
- clear varnish and brush
- fine glass paper
- a damp rag

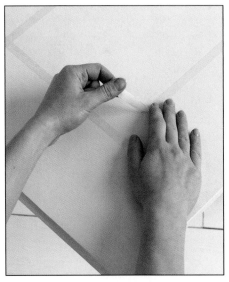

1 Using masking tape, mask off a 30 x 20cm/12 x 8in rectangle on the centre of the table. Make sure that all the corners are right angles using a set square (triangle) and adjust the tapes if necessary.

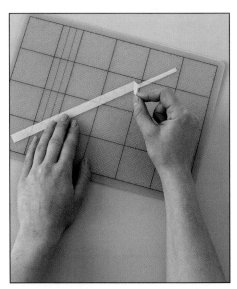

2 Apply lengths of masking tape in rows across the rectangle to make stripes of various widths. Cut some lengths 5mm/¼in wide. To do this, stick the tape to a cutting mat and use a craft knife to cut the tape lengthwise in half, cutting against a metal ruler. Peel the tapes off the mat.

3 Using a flat paintbrush, spread the pale blue, apricot, aquamarine and lilac paints on to a ceramic tile. Dab at the paint with a stencil brush and stencil the stripes in different colours. To stop the paint straying over the 6mm/¼in wide tape, hold a piece of card over the next stripes. Leave the paint to dry then carefully pull off the tapes.

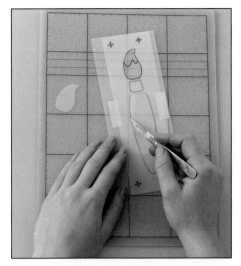

**4** Trace the pencil templates at the back of the book. Tape a piece of stencil card to the tracings. Using the craft knife and cutting mat cut out the stencils, cutting straight lines against a metal ruler. You will need two pencil stencils – the wood, then the pencil and lead. You will need two paintbrush stencils – the handle and bristles, then the metal band and paint.

**5** Lay the pencil stencils together on the table, matching the registration marks along two adjacent sides of the stripes. Tape the pencil wood stencil in place. Mark the registration marks with a soft pencil. Using a flat paintbrush, spread apricot paint on to a ceramic tile. Dab at the paint with a stencil brush. Stencil the pencil woods with apricot paint. Leave to dry.

**6** Move the stencil to the other sides of the stripes, matching up the registration marks. Stencil the pencil woods with apricot acrylic paint as before. Leave to dry completely then remove the stencil.

**7** With masking tape, secure the pencil and lead stencil to the table, matching up the registration marks exactly. Stencil the pencils and leads using lilac, aquamarine and pale blue acrylic paint. Protect the next pencil from any stray paint with a piece of card when stencilling the leads and ends of the pencils. Leave it to dry completely then move the stencil to the other side of the stripes and continue working.

**8** Apply masking tape in rows across the chair seat, making some of the lengths of tape 5mm/¼in wide as before. Mask off the bottom of the chair back and around the edges of the seat.

9 Stencil the seat in coloured stripes to match the table using blue, purple, apricot and an aquamarine paint. Leave the paint to dry completely then peel off the tapes.

10 Tape the paintbrush handle and bristles stencil to the top rail of the chair. Mark the registration marks. Stencil the bristles using apricot paint and stencil the handle.

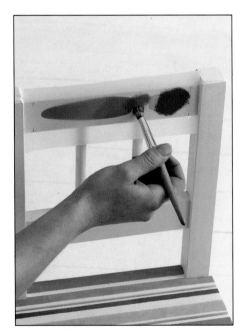

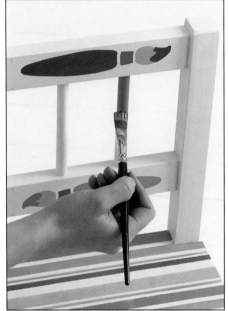

11 Tape the band and paint stencil to the top rail, matching the registration marks. Stencil the band with grey paint. Stencil the paint in a different colour. Repeat on the other rail but turn the stencil so the paintbrush is pointing in the other direction and then use different colours for the handle and paint.

12 Paint any rungs on the chair to co-ordinate with the stripes. Leave to dry then erase the registration marks. Apply two coats of clear varnish, sanding the furniture and wiping it with a damp rag between coats. This will help protect the table and chairs from wear and tear.

# FLOWER POWER CHAIR

Recalling the bright floral patterns of the sixties, this colourful chair will cheer up any kitchen, bedroom or bathroom. Only the seat is decorated, giving the impression that it is covered in a vintage patterned fabric.

1 Sand down the chair seat with medium then fine-grade abrasive paper to prepare the surface for painting, paying special attention to any chips or scratches. Sand the legs, struts and back of the chair in the same way. You may need to repair any deep holes with wood filler.

2 Paint the whole chair with white primer. Leave to dry. Trace the templates at the back of the book and tape them on to stencil card. Cut out, using a craft knife and cutting mat. Trim the edges, leaving a small margin around the motifs, so that the stencil can be positioned close to the struts.

3 Stencil the first flower in blue, using a blocking technique and a fine dry brush. Stencil a sprinkling of blue flowers across the seat, spacing them regularly and altering the angle of each one. Make sure that you have enough space between them to fit in the pink flowers and the tiny green flowers. If you wish, you can mark the positions in with pencil before you start stencilling, to be sure that the spacing is correct.

4 Fill in some of the spaces either side of the blue stencilled flowers with pink acrylic paint, using the same stencil cut out.

5 Using the same paint colours, stencil a few part flowers to overlap the edges of the seat.

6 Add yellow dots in the centre of the large flowers with the small round stencil, dabbing the brush lightly to give a slight texture.

7 Using the small flower stencil, add a few small green flowers in the remaining spaces. Leave to dry completely then protect the seat with two or three coats of matt (flat) varnish. Paint the back and legs of the chair with white wood paint. If your chair has a large flat area across the top edge or wide struts, you could add more flowers to the back. Stencilling and painting four or six different chairs in this way would give you an attractive mismatching set for a modern kitchen or dining room.

RIGHT: Enliven an old kitchen chair by using bright, fresh colours and motifs.

# ORGANZA CUSHION

If you always thought stencilling had a simple country look, then think again. This beautiful organza cushion with gold stencilling takes the craft into the luxury class. Use the sharpest dressmaking pins when handling organza to avoid marking the fabric.

## You will need

- dressmaker's graph paper
- ruler
- pencil
- scissors
- dressmaking pins
- 1m/39in each in main colour and contrast colour organza
- stencil card
- craft knife and self-healing cutting mat
- spray mount
- paper
- masking tape
- gold spray paint
- needle and thread
- sewing machine
- iron
- 50cm/20in cushion pad

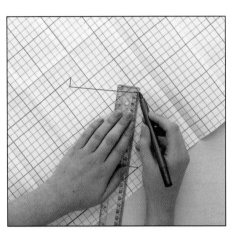

1 Copy the border template at the back of the book on to dressmaker's graph paper and cut out. In addition, cut out a 52cm/21in square and a 52 x 40cm/21 x 16in rectangle from graph paper.

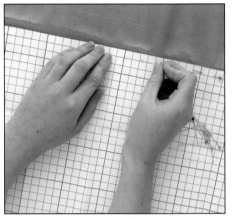

2 Pin the square and rectangle to the main colour organza. Cut two 52cm/21in squares, and two rectangles measuring 52 x 40cm/21 x 16in from the main fabric. Cut four border pieces from the contrasting fabric.

3 Cut a piece of stencil card 18 x 52cm/7 x 21in. Trace the template and transfer to the card, 8cm/3¼in from the bottom edge and with 6cm/2½in to spare at each end. Cut out the stencil using a craft knife and a self-healing cutting mat.

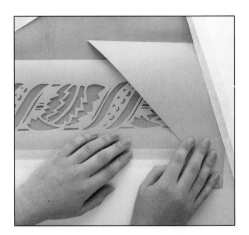

4 Spray the back of the stencil with spray mount and position along the edge of the main organza fabric square. Cut two 45-degree mitres from stencil card, spray with adhesive and press in place. Mask off the surrounding areas with paper.

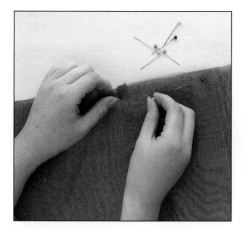

5 Spray with gold paint. Leave to
dry and spray again. Remove
the masking paper and stencil. Place the
stencil along the next edge, put the
mitres in place and continue as before.
Stencil the remaining two sides. Hem one
long edge of each fabric rectangle by
folding over 1cm/$^{1}$/$_{2}$in, then 1.5cm/$^{5}$/$_{8}$in.
Pin, tack (baste) and machine stitch the
hem, then press.

6 Lay the stencilled fabric square face
down and the second square on top.
Lay the two rectangles on top of these
squares, overlapping the stitched edges
so that the raw edges line up with the
square pieces. Pin, tack and machine
stitch 1cm/$^{1}$/$_{2}$in from the raw edge.
Trim the seam allowance to 5mm/$^{1}$/$_{4}$in.
Then, pin, tack and stitch the border
pieces together at the mitred corners
1cm/$^{1}$/$_{2}$in from the raw edges. Trim the
corners and turn the material the right
way out. Press the fabric with a
protective cloth. Continue until the
border pieces make a ring.

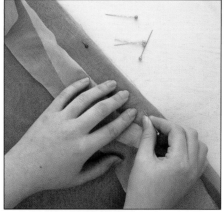

7 Using a protective cloth, press
one of the raw edges under by
1cm/$^{1}$/$_{2}$in. Lay the pressed edge of
the border fabric along the edge of the
main fabric square and pin, tack and
stitch in place.

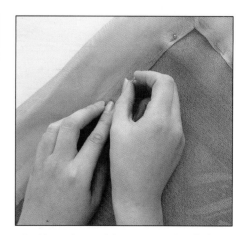

8 Turn the cushion over and pull the
border over. Turn under the border's
raw edge by 1cm/$^{1}$/$_{2}$in and pin in place
along the front of the cushion. Them
tack and stitch in place. Press and insert
the cushion pad.

# FIFTIES ROSE CUSHIONS

Reminiscent of the stylized designs of the 1950s, these rose print cushions would look at home in a classic or contemporary setting. Use your imagination to create more variations on the theme and alter the number of roses on each cushion.

1 Wash the fabric to remove any dressing and press to remove any creases before cutting out the panels. Place the first panel on a pad of newspaper to absorb paint, then check the position of the stencil by placing it over the square.

2 Cut out the stalk and four flower head stencils from acetate using a heat knife or an ordinary craft knife. Spray the reverse of the large rose background stencil with spray mount, then position it towards the top left corner. Block it in with coral paint, using a dry stencil brush.

3 Leave the paint to dry completely, then line up the large petal stencil over the background. Fill it in with a small amount of aubergine paint to complete the rose.

4 Spray the back of the stalk stencil and place it diagonally across the fabric. Fill it in with dark green fabric paint, again loading the brush with the minimum amount to prevent seepage.

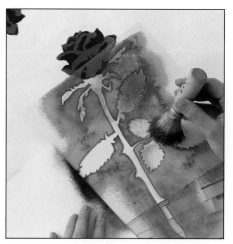

5 The design on the second cushion cover consists of one large and two small roses. Stencil in the rose backgrounds first using coral paint, positioning them so that they point towards the centre of the cushion.

6 Using aubergine paint, add the second layer (the petal stencil) to each of the roses. Line the stencils up by eye so that they fit within the area already painted, and secure in place with spray mount.

7 Stencil in the stalks, allowing the lower part of each one to overlap the edge of the fabric. Leave to dry, then iron both covers on the back to fix (set) the paint, following the instructions supplied by the manufacturer.

8 To make up each cushion cover, stitch a narrow seam along one long edge of the two back panels. With right sides facing and the three raw edges lined up, place one at each side of the front panel so that the seams overlap. Pin and tack (baste) in place, then machine stitch 1cm/½in from the outside edge. Clip the surplus fabric from the corners and ease the corners into shape with the point of a pencil. Turn through and press using a cloth to protect the stencilled side of the cover, then insert the square cushion pad through the opening.

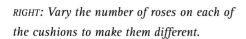

RIGHT: *Vary the number of roses on each of the cushions to make them different.*

# DRAGONFLY CURTAIN

Beautiful, fragile dragonflies hover on this delicate muslin (cheesecloth) curtain. The wing tips of the dragonflies are shaded in a contrasting colour and the insects are stencilled singly and in groups of three.

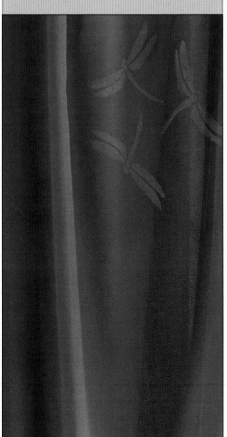

1 Trace the template at the back of the book. Attach a piece of acetate to the tracing with masking tape. Cut out the stencil using a craft knife and self-healing cutting mat, cutting carefully around the acute curved edges.

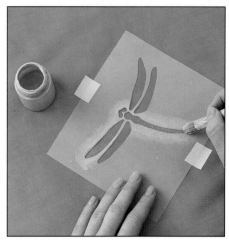

2 Iron the curtain to remove creases. Lay a section of the curtain out flat on a plastic carrier bag, to protect the work surface. Tape the stencil smoothly to the fabric with masking tape. Stencil the dragonfly with lilac fabric paint. Leave to dry.

3 Stencil the tips of the dragonfly wings with aquamarine paint. Leave to dry then remove the stencil.

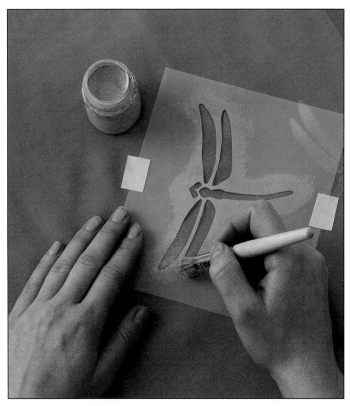

4 Move the stencil to the next position, close to the first dragonfly but not touching it. Tape it in place and stencil as before.

5 When the paint is dry, move the stencil again so that the dragonflies are positioned to "hover" in a group of three. Stencil the third dragonfly.

6 Move the stencil and place it at random on the curtain. Stencil a single dragonfly. Continue stencilling dragonflies all over the curtain in groups of three and singly.

7 Leave the paint to dry overnight then iron the curtain on the wrong side to fix (set) the paint, following the manufacturer's instructions.

# RAINFOREST CURTAINS

Both the positive and negative parts of this stencil are used to create a sophisticated pattern from a single, almost abstract motif. Light streaming through the unlined cotton enhances the hothouse look of this design.

1 Cut the cotton fabric to required size for the curtains, allowing 5cm/2in seam allowances at the sides and lower edge and 2cm/$^3$/$_4$in at the top. Press under, pin and machine-stitch 2.5cm/1in double hems down each side, then repeat the process for the hem at the bottom of the curtain.

2 Calculate the number of tabs you will need, spacing them about 20cm/8in apart. Cut a rectangle of fabric for each tab, using the template at the back of the book. Fold each rectangle in half lengthways and stitch, with a 1cm/$^1$/$_2$in seam allowance. Open out the seam allowance and pin and stitch across one end of the tab so that the seam lies at the centre.

3 Turn each tab to the right side and press. Pin the raw ends of the material to the right side of each curtain, spacing the tabs evenly along the top. For the facing, cut a 7.5cm/3in strip of fabric the width of the curtain plus 4cm/1 $^1$/$_2$in for seam allowances. Pin the strip to the curtain with right sides together and then machine-stitch the top edge.

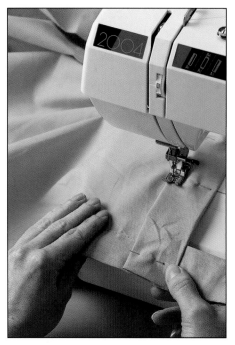

4 Fold the facing to the wrong side, fold in the seam allowances at each end and along the raw edge and then pin in place.

5 Machine-stitch the facing close to the folded edge.

6 Fold the tabs over on to the front side of the curtain and then hand-stitch one of the buttons to hold each tab in place.

7 Enlarge the stencil template at the back of the book on a photocopier to your desired size. Cut a square of acetate sheet the size of the design and fasten it to the design with tabs of masking tape. Cut out using a craft knife and cutting mat. Retain the cut-out part of the stencil for the negative images.

8 Using tailor's chalk, mark the curtains into squares the same size as the stencil. Protect the work surface. Using spray mount, attach the stencil in place in the first marked square. Apply fabric paint with the stencil brush to create a mottled effect. Leave the stencil in place. To make the negative image, mask off the areas around the square with tape.

9 Use spray mount to fix the cut-out motif in the centre, then apply green fabric paint all around it. Remove the stencil and move it to the next marked square. Repeat this pattern all over the curtain. Leave to dry completely then iron the curtain on the wrong side to fix (set) the paint following the manufacturer's instructions.

# ZODIAC CAFÉ CURTAIN

Use gold fabric paints to dramatize a plain muslin (cheesecloth) curtain. Paint the shapes at random on the curtain, but try to plan your design so that they all appear frequently. Add variety by blending the two shades of gold on some of the designs.

### You will need

- tracing paper and pen
- stencil card
- craft knife and self-healing cutting mat
- kitchen paper
- newspaper
- white muslin (cheesecloth), to fit window
- iron
- masking tape
- spray mount
- fabric paints in light and dark gold
- stencil brushes
- sewing machine
- matching thread
- curtain clips and metal rings

1 Trace the stencil motifs from the back of the book. Transfer on to 12 rectangles of stencil card and cut out using a craft knife and cutting mat. Practise your stencilling technique on some spare fabric. Don't overload your brush and wipe off any excess paint on kitchen paper before you begin.

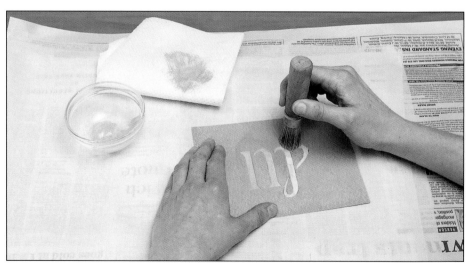

2 Cover your work table with newspaper. Iron the muslin, then tape one corner to the table with masking tape, keeping it flat. Coat the back of each stencil lightly with spray mount before positioning it on the fabric. Stencil with the light gold fabric paint, then stencil over the edges of the motif with dark gold to give depth. Leave to dry, then gently peel the stencil off.

3 Cover the rest of the fabric with the zodiac motifs, repositioning it on the work table as necessary and stencilling one section at a time. Leave to dry then iron the curtain on the wrong side to fix (set) the paints according to the manufacturer's instructions. Hem the edges and attach the curtain clips to the upper edge of the material.

BELOW: *You can change the colours of the zodiac symbols to suit your existing colour scheme if you wish.*

# CITRUS ROLLER BLIND

The stylized, almost abstract, oranges and lemons on this stencilled blind (shade) give it a fifties feel. It would look great in a kitchen decorated with strong, fresh colours.

### You will need

- tracing paper and pen
- stencil card
- craft knife and self-healing cutting mat
- plain white cotton fabric, to fit window
- newspaper
- masking tape
- acrylic gouache paints in orange, yellow, lime green, black and red
- stencil brushes
- fabric stiffener spray
- large decorator's paintbrush
- roller blind (shade) kit

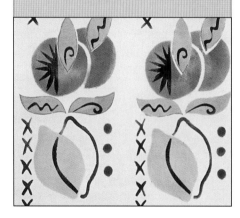

1 Enlarge the template at the back of the book on a photocopier so that the repeat design will fit across the width of your blind (shade) and trace it. Transfer it three times on to stencil card. Using a craft knife and cutting mat, cut out only the areas you will need for each stencil: (1) the lemons, oranges and red spots; (2) the leaves; (3) the black details.

2 Lay out the white cotton fabric on the work surface, covered with newspaper, and secure with masking tape. Using gouache paints, carefully stencil the oranges and lemons motif all over the fabric. Keep the stencil brush as dry as possible, blotting off excess paint, and clean the stencil if paint starts to bleed under the edges.

3 Leave the orange and lemon motifs to dry, then proceed with the remaining colours. Stencil the leaves next, then the red spots (using the first stencil) and finally the black details. Leave to dry then spray the fabric with fabric stiffener following the manufacturer's instructions and hang on a washing line to dry, keeping it straight. Make up the blind using the blind kit.

# GARDEN SHADOWS BLIND

Recreate a bright summer's day in the garden on the gloomiest of dull winter mornings with the beautiful patterns formed as shafts of sunlight cast shadows from clematis and jasmine climbing plants on to a white wall.

### You will need

- closely woven white cotton fabric such as ticking, 30cm/12in deeper and 15cm/6in wider than the window
- iron
- newspaper
- large sheet of acetate
- sheet of glass
- heat knife
- spray mount
- silver fabric paint
- stencil brush
- fabric stiffener spray
- tape measure
- ruler and pencil
- set square
- roller blind (shade) kit
- hacksaw
- abrasive paper (optional)

1 Wash and iron the fabric then place it on a pad of newspaper. Cut out the templates at the back of the book from acetate. Starting at the top centre edge, fix the clematis stencil in place with a light spray of adhesive. Stencil it in with silver fabric paint.

2 Moving down the fabric, stencil a second spray of clematis so that it appears to be joined on to the first. Add another long clematis spray in the same way, just to one side. Use only a small amount of paint at a time to prevent seepage, and build up two or three thin layers of paint to give solid colour.

3 Stencil in a spray of jasmine on the other side, starting it again at the top edge. This will give a denser look to the top part of the design, with the other tendrils trailing down from a leafy branch.

4 Continue stencilling until the fabric is covered, keeping the bottom part less densely patterned with just a few stems trailing down towards the edge.

5 Leave the fabric to dry completely. Fix (set) the paint according to the manufacturer's instructions using a hot iron and coat it with fabric stiffener, again following the manufacturer's instructions supplied.

6 Check the width of the finished blind (shade) once again against the actual window space, then trim the two side edges to this measurement. Mark in the cutting lines with a set square and ruler so that they are straight.

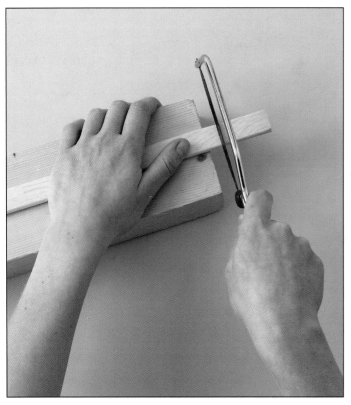

7 Using a hacksaw, cut the wooden batten (furring strip) so that it is 1cm/½in shorter than the finished width of the blind. Sand the ends to neaten, if necessary.

8 Following the directions given with the blind kit, press and stitch a channel along the lower edge. Insert the batten into the channel.

9 Cut the wooden roller to size and attach the metal fittings as directed. Fix the top edge of the blind to the adhesive tape supplied on the roller. Add the tacks if necessary to secure it in place.

10 Knot the acorn on to the cord, then thread the other end through the oval metal plate as shown in the instructions. Screw it in place at the centre back of the batten, then fix the blind to the window.

# ROSE TABLECLOTH

Two stencils are arranged here to decorate a square tablecloth; the same motifs could be used in many different combinations and sizes. Use two or three shades with each stencil shape to give a rounded, three-dimensional look to the roses, leaves and branches.

### You will need

- tracing paper and pen
- stencil card or acetate
- craft knife and self-healing cutting mat
- 76cm/30in square of heavy white cotton fabric
- iron
- newspaper
- spray mount
- fabric paints in dark pink, pale pink, yellow, dark green, light green and warm brown
- stencil brushes
- vanishing fabric marker
- long ruler and T-square
- sewing machine
- white sewing thread

1 Enlarge the rose template at the back of the book on a photocopier so that it measures 15cm/6in across. Enlarge the branch template so that it is 30cm/12in long. Transfer both on to stencil card or acetate and carefully cut out using a craft knife and self-healing cutting mat.

2 Cover the work surface with newspaper. Fold the fabric in half each way, to find the centre. Press lightly along the creases. Spray the back of the rose stencil with spray mount and place it in the middle of the cloth. Stencil the rose, starting with dark pink paint in the corner petals and around the outer edge of the inner petals.

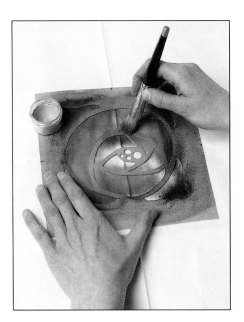

3 Fill in the rest of the petals with pale pink and colour the centre dots in yellow. Keep the brush upright and use a small circling motion to transfer the paint. Be careful not to overload the bristles. Peel off the stencil and allow the paint to dry.

4 Work a branch motif on each side of the rose, using the crease as a placement guide, to form a cross. Spray the back of the card with adhesive, as before. Stencil yellow paint in the centre of each leaf. ▶

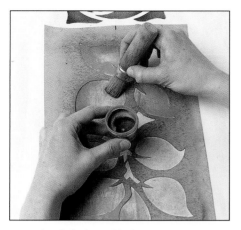

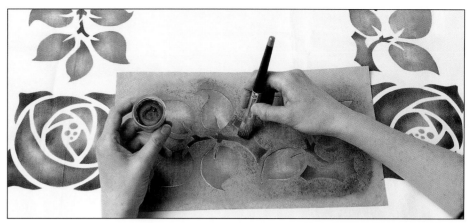

5 Blend dark and light green paint and finish painting the leaves.

6 Work a small amount of brown fabric paint around the base of the leaves and the outside edge of the branches. Stencil a rose at the end of each branch. With a vanishing fabric marker, and using the ruler and T-square to get a perfectly accurate square, draw a line about 15cm/6in from each edge so that it is on the same level as the outer edge of the roses. Stencil a rose in each corner and then work a branch between the roses.

7 Leave the paint to dry then iron the tablecloth on the wrong side to fix (set) according to the manufacturer's instructions. To finish the tablecloth, turn under, press and stitch a narrow double hem along the outside edge.

*BELOW: If your tablecloth is larger than 76cm/30in, add in more rows of this stencilled rose pattern to fit the size of your chosen cloth.*

# SUMMER QUILT COVER

A combination of stencilling and sponging is used to decorate this ready-made duvet cover. Choose light colours for the stripes so that the stencilling will show up.

## You will need

- newspaper
- pale-coloured duvet cover, pre-washed
- dressmaking pins
- iron
- tracing paper and pen
- acetate or stencil card
- magic marker
- craft knife and self-healing cutting mat
- tailor's chalk
- string
- fabric paints in pink, green and yellow
- large household sponge
- spray mount
- small sponges or stencil brushes
- sewing machine

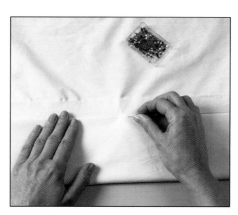

**1** Cover the work surface with newspaper. Protect the back of the duvet cover from paint bleeding through by unpicking the sides of the cover and opening it out into a large rectangle. Roll up the underside of the cover and pin it so that it is out of the way. Lay out the upper side of the duvet with the area to be painted ironed flat.

**2** Enlarge the templates at the back of the book on a photocopier, to suit your design. Trace on to stencil card and cut out using a craft knife and a self-healing cutting mat.

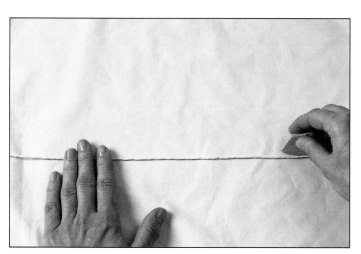

**3** Using tailor's chalk, mark stripes across the duvet. First mark the position of the stripes at the edge of the duvet, making them deep enough for the stencils to fit. Then mark the midpoint on each stripe. Using a piece of string stretched across the duvet and pinned at each side, rule these lines across.

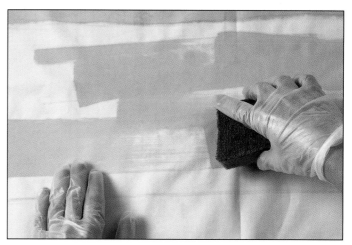

**4** Dilute the fabric paint with water to the consistency of ink. Using the large household sponge, fill in the stripes of colour. Do not worry if the edges are a little rough, because this will make the final effect look more interesting. Leave each section of paint to dry before moving on to the next.

5 When the whole area is painted and completely dry, iron the fabric on the reverse to fix (set) the paint according to the manufacturer's instructions.

6 Spray the reverse of a stencil with spray mount. Place it on the midpoint of a stripe and apply colours using a small sponge or stencil brush.

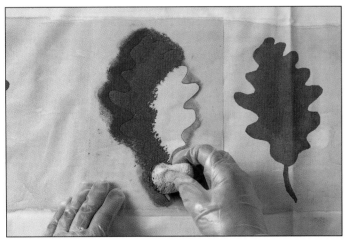

7 Continue to stencil, keeping the motifs evenly spaced. After removing each stencil from the fabric, wipe away the excess paint to keep the colours clean.

8 Try blending colours together to give the finished stencil a textured appearance.

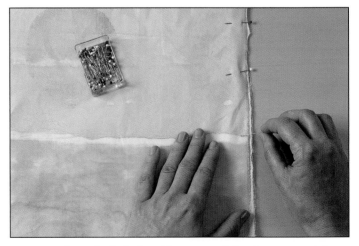

9 When the stencilling has been completed and the paint is thoroughly dry, iron again on the wrong side to fix (set) the paints according to the manufacturer's instructions.

10 Pin and stitch the side seams of the duvet cover. The fabric may seem stiff at first but washing it should solve this.

# FEATHER THROW

The fringed border of this beautiful throw is created by simply pulling away the woven threads along each edge. Choose a fabric with a square, rather than a twill, weave that can easily be unravelled. Linen or heavy cotton would be ideal.

### You will need

- iron
- approximately 1.3m/50in square of cream furnishing fabric
- tape measure
- scissors
- carbon paper and sharp pencil
- stencil card
- craft knife and self-healing cutting mat
- spray mount
- fabric paints in brown and white
- saucer
- large stencil brush
- pressing cloth

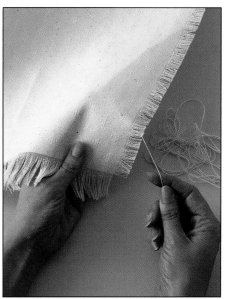

1 Wash the fabric to remove any chemical residue and press it well. Cut it into a perfect 1.3m/50in square by snipping between the threads to get a straight line along each edge.

2 To make the fringed edging, carefully unravel the fabric, one thread at a time, for a distance of 4cm/1½in along each side.

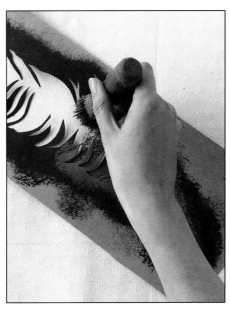

3 Enlarge the template at the back of the book on a photocopier and transfer it on to the stencil card using carbon paper. Cut it out, using a sharp craft knife and self-healing cutting mat. Spray the back lightly with spray mount and place it on the first corner. Mix a small amount of white and brown fabric paint in a saucer and stipple the feather with a dry brush.

4 Repeat the motif at roughly regular intervals across the
fabric, altering the angle of the stencil so that the feathers
are positioned randomly. Mix two shades of brown paint to
make some of them light and others slightly darker, giving
variety to the pattern.

5 Following the manufacturer's instructions, fix (set) the
paint by ironing it with a hot steam iron and pressing cloth.

*RIGHT: This throw is made from an upholstery-weight fabric,
which gives it a rather heavy look, ideal to go across the arm of
a chair or back of a sofa. Stencilling on to organza or a metallic
voile would make a much more ethereal version to drape over a
romantically dressed bed or to hang at a window.*

# LOVE PILLOWS

Make sure the message gets across by stencilling the word "love" on your pillows in both English and French. The typeface used is Gill Sans Bold, enlarged here to 42.5cm/17in long. Always pre-wash and iron the fabric to remove any glazes that could block the colour absorption.

### You will need

- spray mount
- 2 pieces of stencil card
- craft knife and self-healing cutting mat
- sheet of thin card (stock)
- white cotton pillowcases
- red fabric paint
- plate
- stencil brush
- iron

1 Enlarge the templates at the back of the book to the required size on a photocopier. Coat the backs of the photocopies with spray mount and stick them to the stencil card.

2 Cut out the letters using a craft knife and cutting mat. The O, A and R need ties to retain the internal letter features, so draw in "bridges" before you cut out the letters.

3 Place a sheet of thick card (stock) inside the pillowcase, so that the paint colour does not bleed through to the other side.

4 Stencil the letters. Leave to dry then remove the card and iron the pillow cases on the reverse side to set the paint following the manufacturer's instructions.

# SEASHELL BEACH BAG

Crisp cream and navy give this smart beach bag a nautical look. Much of the charm of the stencilling lies in combining colours to give a three-dimensional look to the seashell shapes, so it's worth practising on spare fabric or lining paper first.

## You will need

- iron
- 55 x 75cm/21½ x 30in cream cotton drill fabric
- scissors
- tracing paper and pen
- stencil card
- craft knife and self-healing cutting mat
- spray mount
- 2 lengths of blue cotton drill fabric or denim, each 15 x 38cm/6 x 15in
- fabric paints in dark yellow, dark red and navy blue
- stencil brushes
- sewing machine
- white, dark orange and blue sewing threads
- dressmaking pins
- 2m/6ft cream cotton cord
- masking tape

1 Wash and iron the cream fabric then cut in two lengthways. Trace the stencil from the back of the book or enlarge it on a photocopier. Transfer the outline to stencil card and cut out using a craft knife and cutting mat. Coat the back lightly with spray mount, and stencil five shells on each piece of fabric, using two or three colours. Leave to dry then iron on the reverse side to fix (set) the paint according to the manufacturer's instructions.

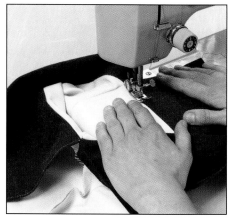

2 With the fabric right sides together, stitch a blue strip to the top edge of each cream piece, leaving a 1cm/½in seam allowance. Press the seam upward. Pin the rectangles right sides together, and stitch around the main bag. Press under the seam allowances on the open sides of the blue fabric, and topstitch in orange sewing thread. Fold in half lengthways. Machine-stitch parallel to the topstitch.

3 Cut the cord in half, and bind the ends with masking tape. Thread both pieces through the bag. Remove the tape, and bind the ends with blue thread, 5cm/2in from the ends. Fringe and comb the cord to make tassels. Trim neatly.

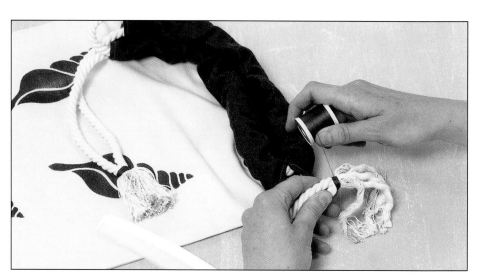

*OPPOSITE: The choice of navy blue and red gives this beach bag a nautical look.*

# GINGERBREAD APRON

This apron wraps right around the waist so will protect clothing from the stickiest of fingers. The gingerbread pattern is so appealing there will be no question about young chefs wanting to put it on before creating their culinary masterpieces.

## You will need

- cream cotton fabric, height the distance from the child's collar to the knee and width the child's waist measurement
- iron
- pencil
- scissors
- sewing needle and thread
- sewing machine
- cream thread
- tracing paper and pen or carbon paper and sharp pencil
- masking tape
- stencil card
- craft knife and self-healing cutting mat
- newspaper
- stencil brush
- fabric paints in ochre, brown, black and red
- fine artist's paintbrush
- 1m/30in of 2.5cm/1in-wide cream or white ribbon or tape

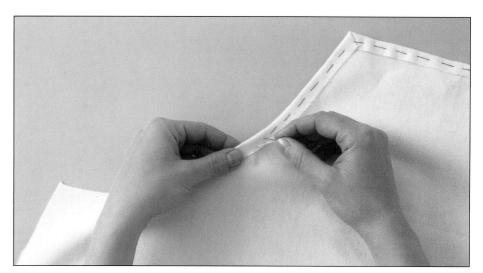

1 Wash and press the fabric. Fold it in half widthways and mark the child's waist position at the side edges. Mark a point 7.5cm/3in from the fold at the top edge and draw a curve between these two points. Cut along this curve, through both layers of fabric. Check the size against the child and alter if necessary. Neaten the cut edges with a 1cm/½in seam. Tack (baste) then machine stitch.

2 Fold the apron in half widthways again and press along the crease, then press a turning about 12cm/4½in from the bottom edge. These creases will act as a guide for positioning the stencil.

3 Trace the template at the back of the book and tape it on to stencil card. Using a craft knife and cutting mat, cut it out. Place the fabric on a layer of newspaper. Position the stencil in the centre of the apron so that the feet touch the horizontal crease. Using a dry brush, stipple it in with a light layer of ochre paint.

4 Add a stippling of brown paint around the edges of the stencil to give a more three-dimensional look to the gingerbread figure. Any irregularities in the surface will add to the cookie-like texture, so the paint does not have to be too smooth or densely applied.

5 Stencil in another two gingerbread figures at either side, varying the density of colour in each one to give them an individual appearance. Keep their feet along the crease so that they stand in a straight row. Measure the distance between their hands before positioning the stencil to make sure they are evenly spaced.

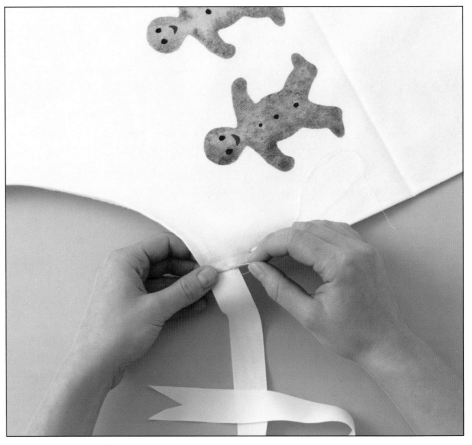

6 Using a fine artist's paintbrush, paint in two black "currant" circles for the eyes and a red semicircular "cherry slice" mouth to complete the face on the gingerbread men. Each one can have their own individual expression if you wish. Paint three "currant" buttons down their bodies. Leave to dry completely, then iron the apron on the reverse to fix (set) the paint, following the manufacturer's instructions.

7 Cut two 30cm/12in lengths of ribbon and trim one end of each into a fishtail shape. Stitch the other ends in position at the waist. Stitch the remaining ribbon in a loop at the neck.

# AMISH FLOORCLOTH

Floorcloths were very popular in America during the 18th century, using painted sailcloth canvas to imitate chequered marble floors or the geometric designs of oriental carpets. The pattern for this floorcloth is adapted from an Amish quilt and the colours are also Amish-inspired, but you can use any combination.

## You will need

- 1.5m x 90cm/5ft x 3ft heavy artist's canvas
- staple gun (optional)
- white acrylic primer or matt emulsion (flat latex) paint
- medium decorator's paintbrush
- medium-grade abrasive paper
- ruler and pencil
- strong fabric adhesive
- metal spoon
- acetate sheet or stencil card
- craft knife and self-healing cutting mat
- spray mount
- artist's acrylics or stencil paints in blue, brick red, purple, light blue, dusky pink and light emerald green
- stencil brushes
- clear water-based varnish and brush
- small tubes of artist's acrylic paint in raw umber and raw sienna

1 Turn the canvas over. If you want to secure it, staple it down. Apply three coats of primer or emulsion (latex) paint, rubbing lightly with abrasive paper between coats.

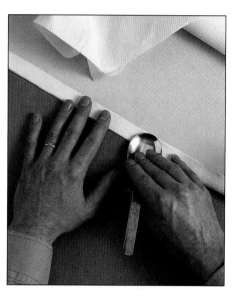

2 Using a ruler and pencil, draw a border 4cm/1½in wide around the edge, mitring the corners. Apply strong fabric adhesive to the border and fold it flat, using the back of a spoon to apply pressure and smooth any bumps.

3 Mark out the design from the back of the book except for the stars. Paint the framework following the colour scheme illustrated.

4 Cut three simple geometric stencils following the design at the back of the book from acetate sheet or stencil card using a sharp craft knife and self-healing cutting mat.

5 Stencil the red and blue stars in the centre of the large squares. Give the back of the stencil a light coat of spray mount to keep it in place as you paint. Use the paint sparingly on a dry brush but try to get a flat colour finish.

6 When the stars are dry add the purple and light blue triangles. Lightly spray the back of the stencil with adhesive and place it over the star, aligning the white space with the stencil cut-out.

7 The corner boxes are done in alternate colours. Begin by painting half of them using dusky pink acrylic or stencil paint and a medium-to-large stencil brush.

8 Finish the colour scheme for the floorcloth by painting the rest of the corner boxes with light emerald green acrylic or stencil paint.

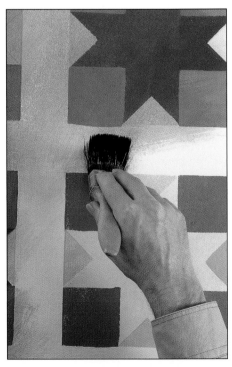

9 Apply one coat of varnish tinted with a squeeze of raw umber and raw sienna acrylic paint to mellow the colour. Leave to dry then apply two coats of clear varnish, allowing adequate drying time between them.

# GILDED LAMPSHADE

A simple parchment lampshade makes an ideal base for gilding. The heraldic stencilled design on a shellac base coat gives the shade an antique appearance. Use a low-wattage bulb with this shade to avoid tarnishing.

1 Using a large round stencil brush, stipple an even but blotchy coat of amber shellac varnish over the surface of the lampshade. Leave to dry for 30 minutes to 1 hour.

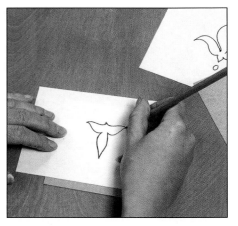

2 Trace the templates from the back of the book and transfer to stencil card or acetate.

3 Cut out the stencils using a craft knife and cutting mat.

4 Mark the positions for the stencils around the lampshade. Secure the first stencil at the bottom of the shade with masking tape. Stir the gold paint well, then stipple through the stencil. Do not load the brush with too much paint or it will bleed. Remove the stencil carefully before repositioning it.

5 When you have completed the bottom row, secure the second stencil at the top of the shade. Stencil the top row in the same way as before. Leave the shade to dry for at least 1 hour.

*OPPOSITE: You could try using silver, bronze or pewter stencil paint on this lampshade.*

# ELIZABETHAN LAMPSHADE

Here, an Elizabethan border design is applied to a lampshade using a combination of sponge and stencil techniques. The pattern would also look sumptuous using deep blue or red with gold. For a larger lampshade, enlarge the template on a photocopier.

1 Trace the template at the back of the book on to the acetate sheet. Cut out using a craft knife and cutting mat or a heat knife.

2 Lay the design on a sheet of white paper and, using a stencil brush, apply undiluted black paint to the paper around the acetate. Keep the brush upright and dab, rather than brush, the paint on.

3 Apply the base colours of gold and white to the lampshade using a sponge. Take up only a small amount of paint each time, so that the texture of the sponge is transferred to the shade. Leave to dry.

4 Using strips of low-tack masking tape, attach the stencil to the lampshade. Use small curls of tape on the underside of the stencil to attach parts that do not lay flat.

5 Using the stencil brush, apply small amounts of black paint to the lampshade, gradually building up the density of colour. Remove the stencil and allow the paint to dry. To speed up the drying process, you can use a hairdryer.

6 Tape the stencil to the next position and apply paint as before until the whole lampshade has been patterned. Leave to dry.

7 Retape the stencil to the lampshade, taking care to position the stencil over the previous work. Use a small piece of sponge to apply gold highlights.

# GOLD LEAF PICTURE FRAME

This picture frame has been decorated using a simple square stencil, which has been embellished with gold leaf. Applying leaf metals is a technique that should not be rushed.

## You will need

- craft knife and self-healing cutting mat
- heavy card (stock)
- triangle (set square)
- scissors
- canvas, linen or heavy silk
- spray mount
- vanishing fabric pen or soft pencil
- double-sided tape
- needle and thread
- masking tape
- stencil card or acetate film
- deep red fabric paint
- stencil brush or sponge
- gold leaf
- size soft brush
- PVA (white) glue and brush
- clear varnish or lacquer and brush

1 Using a craft knife and a self-healing cutting mat, cut two pieces of card (stock) to the size that you wish your frame to be. Cut a central window in one piece. The frame illustrated here has a total area of 21 x 21cm/8$\frac{1}{2}$ x 8$\frac{1}{2}$in with a central window of 9 x 9cm/3$\frac{1}{2}$ x 3$\frac{1}{2}$in.

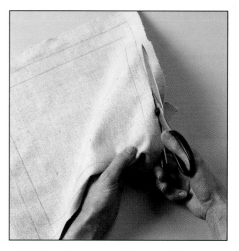

2 Cut out a piece of canvas, linen or heavy silk 2cm/$\frac{3}{4}$in larger all around than the picture frame.

3 Apply spray mount to the frame and place it in the centre of the fabric, wrong side up. Rub your hand over the card to form a secure bond.

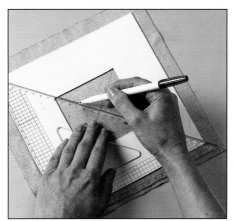

4 Using a vanishing fabric pen or pencil, draw two diagonals across the window. Measure and cut out a 5cm/2in square in the centre of the frame.

5 Apply strips of double-sided tape all round the reverse edges of the frame. Pull the extra fabric back and stick it down. Cut a mitre in each corner and stitch.

6 To keep the back of the frame neat and tidy, apply masking tape over the raw edges of the fabric.

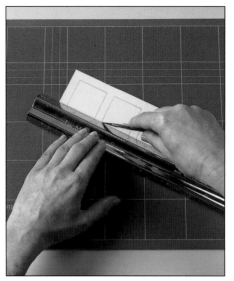

7 Using a craft knife, cut a piece of stencil card or acetate film to a rectangle the same size as one side of the frame, corner to corner (21 x 6cm/8$^{1}/_{2}$ x 2$^{1}/_{2}$in for the frame illustrated). Mark out equally spaced squares along the length (4cm/1$^{1}/_{2}$in squares with a 1cm/$^{1}/_{2}$in division), and cut out.

8 Using masking tape, attach the stencil to one side of the front of the frame. Fill in the squares with colour using a stencil brush or sponge. Leave to dry then remove the stencil and tape it to the next side, matching the corner squares. Continue until all four sides have been coloured.

9 Carefully following the manufacturer's instructions, apply a small gold leaf square inside the stencilled one. Usually, this involves applying size and leaving for 15 minutes before applying the gold leaf with a soft brush. Leave for about 2 hours to set, then buff up the gold leaf and remove the unstuck pieces of gold.

10 Using heavy card and a sharp-bladed craft knife, cut out a right-angled triangle of the same height as the frame and 10cm/4in wide. Score along the longest side 1cm/$^{1}/_{2}$in from the edge and then use PVA (white) glue to stick it to the backing board cut out in step 1.

11 Apply PVA glue to the reverse of the backing board on three sides and stick it to the frame. The top is left open to slide in a picture. To protect the gold leaf and to prevent dust from collecting on the fabric, paint the front of the frame with one or two coats of clear varnish or lacquer.

# FRAMED CHALKBOARD

Once you have had a chalkboard in the kitchen it becomes one of life's absolute essentials. Here the frame is made of an old plank sawn into four pieces – two long, two short glued together. Choose the size to suit your wall space. Cramp the frame while the glue sets or hold it together with string, twisting a pencil in the string to tighten it.

### You will need

- frame made up as above
- tracing paper and pen
- spray mount
- stencil card
- craft knife and self-healing cutting mat
- emulsion (latex) paints in dull blue and red
- small decorator's paintbrush
- medium-grade abrasive paper
- spray mount
- stencil brush
- artist's acrylic paint in black
- antiquing varnish and brush
- hardboard, 2.5cm/1in larger all around than the inner frame measurement
- blackboard paint
- small hammer and panel pins (brads)
- (you will also need a piece of chalk!)

1 Trace the templates, or enlarge them on a photocopier. Spray the back lightly with spray mount and stick on to stencil card. Cut out the shapes using a craft knife and cutting mat.

2 Paint the frame with dull blue emulsion (latex) paint. Leave to dry completely.

3 Paint the inner and outer edges of the frame with red emulsion paint. Leave to dry.

4 Rub the paint with medium-grade abrasive paper to reveal the grain of the wood.

5 Spray the back of each stencil lightly with spray mount and position on the frame. Arrange the shapes as shown in the main picture.

6 Using a small stencil brush, lightly apply the red emulsion paint to the frame.

7 Darken the red paint slightly by mixing in a little black acrylic paint.

8 Using the stencil brush, rub the dark red paint deep into the grain in just a few places.

9 When dry, rub over with abrasive paper to remove any dark red paint from the surface.

10 Apply one or two coats of antiquing varnish. Leave the frame to dry.

*OPPOSITE: The best country accessories usually look worn and loved like this framed chalkboard.*

11 Paint the hardboard with two coats of blackboard paint. Leave to dry.

12 Attach the blackboard to the back of the frame, using panel pins (brads).

# LEAFY PICTURE FRAMES

The stylish raised leaf patterns around these frames are simple to create using ordinary white interior filler instead of paint to fill in the stencilled leaf shapes. The simple shapes can be cut out with scissors.

### You will need

- 2 wooden frames
- dark green acrylic paint
- medium decorator's paintbrush
- fine-grade abrasive paper
- stencil card
- scissors
- ready-mixed interior filler
- stencil brush

1 Paint the frames dark green. When dry, gently rub them down with abrasive paper to create a subtle distressed effect.

2 Enlarge the templates at the back of the book to fit the frames. Transfer the designs to stencil card and cut them out using scissors.

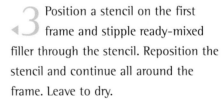

3 Position a stencil on the first frame and stipple ready-mixed filler through the stencil. Reposition the stencil and continue all around the frame. Leave to dry.

4 Repeat with a different combination of motifs on the second frame. When the filler is completely hard, gently smooth over the leaves with abrasive paper.

*OPPOSITE: You can also use textured gel combined with acrylic paint and stippled on to the frame to achieve a similar effect.*

# ART NOUVEAU HATBOX

An elegantly stencilled hatbox and matching shoe bag would be perfect for storing a bride's hat and shoes. Make a set for yourself or to give to someone special. And you needn't stop there: stencil a whole stack of matching hatboxes to use for stylish storage in a bedroom.

## You will need

- round hatbox
- medium decorator's paintbrushes
- white undercoat
- pale green water-based woodwash
- tape measure
- pencil
- tracing paper and pen
- stencil card
- craft knife and self-healing cutting mat
- ruler
- spray mount
- stencil brushes
- stencil paints in dark green, royal blue and pale green

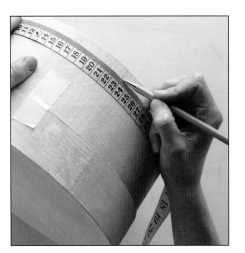

1 Paint the hatbox with two coats of white undercoat. Dilute one part pale green woodwash with one part water and apply two or three light washes to the hatbox, allowing them to dry between coats. Measure the circumference of the box and divide by six or eight. Lightly mark the measurements on the lid and side of the box with a pencil.

2 Trace the flower and heart templates at the back of the book and cut from stencil card. Rule a pencil line across the bottom of the stencil to help align it on the box. Spray with spray mount and position on the box. Using a stencil brush and dark green stencil paint, stencil the leaves and stem. Remove the stencil when dry, respray with spray mount and reposition.

3 Continue to work around the box. Reposition the stencil on the leaves and add shadow to the points where the leaves join the stem, using royal blue paint and a clean brush.

LEFT: *Stencil a matching calico shoe bag to protect a treasured pair of shoes.*

OPPOSITE: *Line a hatbox with matching tissue paper.*

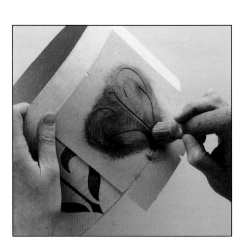

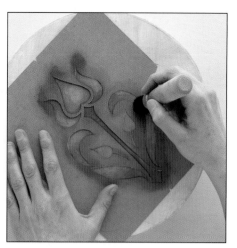

4 Using the single heart stencil, add a pale green heart between each pair of leaves.

5 Stencil flowerheads around the rim of the lid in dark green, adding a royal blue shadow as before. Stencil the flower motif in the centre of the lid.

6 Add pale green heart motifs around the main motif, using a very small amount of paint for a delicate touch.

# CITRUS FRUIT TRAY

This bamboo tray has been given a tropical look with juicy orange and lime stencils, perfect for summer drinks on a sunny day. You could also transform an old tray by painting over the existing surface.

### You will need

- fine-grade abrasive paper
- tray
- tracing paper and pen or carbon paper and sharp pencil
- masking tape
- stencil card
- craft knife and self-healing cutting mat
- acrylic paints in pale orange, dark orange, pale green, dark green, dark brown and white
- stencil brush
- gloss or matt (flat) varnish and brush

1 Sand the tray lightly to remove any existing varnish. Trace the templates at the back of the book and tape on to stencil card. Using a craft knife and cutting mat cut them out, leaving a narrow margin round each motif.

2 Stipple a couple of pale orange circles using a small to medium-size stencil brush, as the background for the orange slices, protecting the surface of the rest of the tray with masking tape.

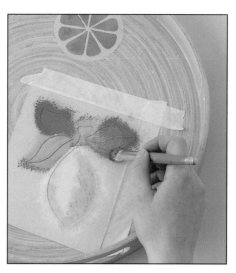

3 Fix the circle stencil back in place over the oranges and slot the segment stencil within it. Using dark orange, fill in the segments, adding some light and dark stippling to create texture within the shapes.

4 Stipple the lime and leaves in two shades of green. Give the fruit a more three-dimensional look by stippling light green in the centre and dark green around the outside edge. Stipple the stalk in dark brown.

5 Stencil the "rind" of the lime segments in dark green and the main part in light green. Add light white stippling across the "pips". Leave to dry completely then apply three coats of gloss or matt (flat) varnish.

# GILDED CANDLES

Church candles look extra special adorned with simple gold stars and stripes. Always associated with Christmas, candles are popular all year round for their soft romantic lighting. Cutting the stencils may be fiddly but it is then a quick job to spray on the gold paint.

### You will need

- acetate
- selection of candles
- marker pen
- tracing paper and pen
- craft knife and self-healing cutting mat
- spray mount
- masking tape
- metallic spray paint
- protective face mask

1 Wrap a piece of acetate around the candle. Mark and cut it to fit exactly. Do not overlap the edges. Cut it a few millimetres shorter than the candle.

2 Trace the star templates at the back of the book. Lay a piece of acetate over the stars and trace over them with a marker pen.

3 Cut out the stars using a craft knife and cutting mat.

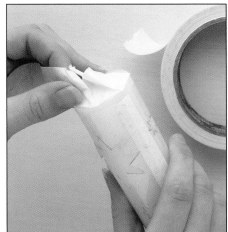

4 Spray one side of the stencil with spray mount and wrap around the candle, centring it so that there is a small gap at either end. Secure the acetate join with masking tape. Mask the top of the candle, ensuring there are no gaps.

*RIGHT:* *Create a range of attractive gilded patterns by varying the size of the stencilled stars and stripes used on the candles.*

5 Spray a very fine mist of metallic spray paint over the candle, holding the can about 30cm/12in from the surface. If too much paint is applied, it will drip underneath the stencil. Keep checking that the stencil is well stuck down to avoid any fuzzy lines around the stars. Leave the paint to dry for a couple of minutes, then carefully remove the masking tape and acetate.

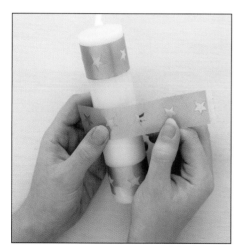

6 For a stars and stripes candle, cut strips of acetate and trace a line of stars along each strip. Cut out as before. Spray one side of the acetate strips with spray mount. Stick the strips on to the candle at equal spaces. Secure them with small pieces of tape at the join.

7 Mask off the top of the candle as before. Spray the candle with metallic paint and remove the masking tape and stencil when dry.

8 For a reverse stencil design, cut out individual star shapes from acetate. Apply spray mount to one side, stick on to the candle and mask off the top of the candle as before. Spray with metallic paint and carefully remove the acetate stars when the paint is dry.

# LEAF-ETCHED VASE

The delicate effect of etched glass is easy to imitate nowadays with a glass etching spray, which is now available from most good art and craft suppliers. For the best results, spray through a stencil cut from adhesive plastic.

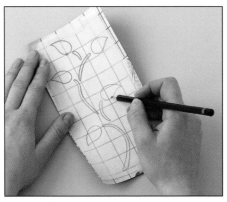

1 Trace the template at the back of the book. Using masking tape, tape the tracing face down on to the back of a piece of sticky-back plastic (contact paper). Draw over the design to transfer it. Cut out the stencil using a craft knife and cutting mat.

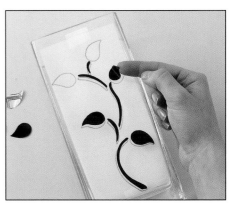

2 Make sure the vase is clean and free from grease. Trim the tracing to fit inside the vase. Tape the tracing inside the front of the vase. Peel the backing paper off the stencils and stick in position on the front of the vase matching the positions on the template.

3 Upturn the vase and slip it over a taller item so the vase rim does not rest on the work surface. Cover the surrounding area with a scrap piece of plastic or paper. Spray the vase with glass etching spray following the manufacturer's instructions.

4 Leave the vase to dry thoroughly and apply a second coat if necessary. Carefully peel off all the stencils. Do not clean the vase in a dishwasher but wash gently in warm soapy water.

# TEMPLATES

The templates on the following pages may be resized to any scale required. The simplest way of doing this is to enlarge them on a photocopier, or trace the design and draw a grid of evenly spaced squares over your tracing. Draw a larger grid on another piece of paper and copy the outline square by square. Draw over the lines to make sure they are continuous.

BRONZE
CHAIR *page*
*32*

SCANDINAVIAN
CHAIR *page 35*

PAINTED
DRAWERS *page 38*

TRAIN TOY
BOX
*page 41*

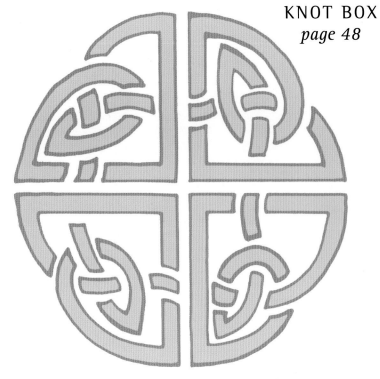

CELTIC
KNOT BOX
*page 48*

HAWAIIAN HIBISCUS
CABINET
*page 44*

DAISY STOOL
*page 51*

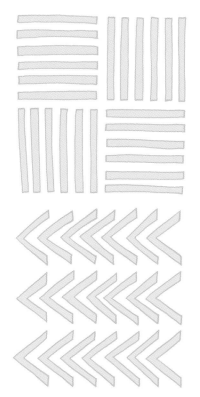

AFRICAN
BEDSIDE
CHEST
*page 57*

STRIPED TABLE AND CHAIRS
*page 60*

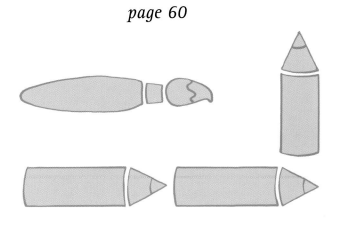

**FLOWER POWER CHAIR**
*page 64*

**ORGANZA CUSHION**
*page 66*

**FIFTIES ROSE CUSHIONS**
*page 68*

**DRAGONFLY CURTAIN**
*page 70*

**RAINFOREST CURTAINS**
*page 73*

**ZODIAC CAFE CURTAIN**
*page 76*

**CITRUS ROLLER BLIND**
*page 78*

GARDEN
SHADOWS
BLIND
*page 80*

ROSE
TABLECLOTH
*page 84*

SUMMER QUILT
COVER
*page 86*

LOVE
PILLOWS
*page 92*

AEOLMRUR

SEASHELL
BEACH
BAG
*page 94*

FEATHER
THROW
*page 89*

GINGERBREAD APRON
*page 96*

## AMISH FLOORCLOTH
*page 99*

## GILDED LAMPSHADE
*page 102*

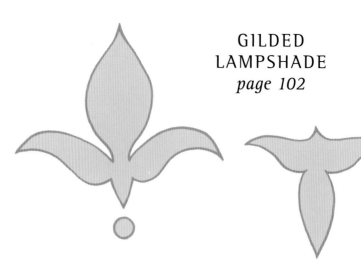

## ELIZABETHAN LAMPSHADE
*page 104*

## FRAMED CHALKBOARD
*page 109*

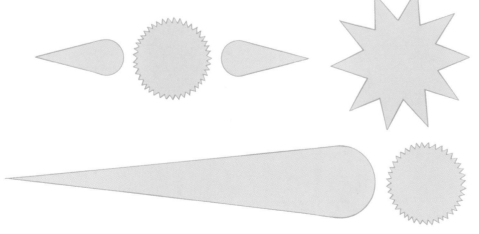

## LEAFY PICTURE FRAMES
*page 112*

ART NOUVEAU
HATBOX
*page 114*

CITRUS
FRUIT
TRAY
*page 116*

LEAF-ETCHED VASE
*page 120*

GILDED
CANDLES
*page 118*

# INDEX